Vaccination & Immunization

Immunization

What does your child need?

Anne Charlish

Thorsons
An Imprint of HarperCollinsPublishers

I am indebted to Anne Johnson
for her very capable assistance with every
aspect of this book.

Thorsons
An Imprint of HarperCollins*Publishers*
77–85 Fulham Palace Road,
Hammersmith, London W6 8JB
1160 Battery Street
San Francisco, California 94111–1213

Published by Thorsons 1996

1 3 5 7 9 10 8 6 4 2

© Anne Charlish 1996

Anne Charlish asserts the moral right to
be identified as the author of this work

A catalogue record for this book
is available from the British Library

ISBN 0 7225 3283 0

Printed in Great Britain by
Caledonian International Book Manufacturing Ltd, Glasgow

Contents

Warning Signs

If your child has any of the following symptoms, you should seek professional medical treatment urgently. If your GP cannot attend without delay, then contact the Accident and Emergency Department at your nearest hospital. Things to look out for include:

- a fever of 38.5°C (101°F) or over
- unexplained, abnormal drowsiness
- convulsions or fits
- a severe headache
- impaired vision, particularly if this is combined with a severe headache
- excessive vomiting or diarrhoea
- a stiff neck, particularly if this is combined with a dislike of bright light (photophobia)
- any severe pain or obvious distress
- refusal to eat food for longer than a day or two

Introduction

The question of whether or not to immunize one's child is a matter of considerable concern for parents. We desperately want to place our trust in immunization. Something that is guaranteed to protect our children's health for the rest of their lives seems to be too good to refuse.

Yet nagging at the back of one's mind is a measure of doubt. We've heard about the possibility of side-effects. We've also heard about some babies being brain-damaged or even dying as a result of immunization. We are now no longer sure that this really is the right thing to do.

There are plenty of people who are very keen to offer their advice and to help you reach a decision. There is your own general practitioner, who will probably do his or her utmost to persuade you that immunization is good not only for your child but for the world as a whole. There is the Government, which will make reassuring noises and fund massive publicity campaigns with the sole aim of encouraging maximum uptake of the immunizations on offer. There are the proponents of natural medicine who will tell you that a child's natural defences are the best ones he or she can hope for and that it is wrong to interfere with them. Then there are the anti-immunization pressure groups, who quickly become evangelical on the subject and offer countless horror stories to put you off the idea of ever immunizing your poor, unsuspecting baby.

And then, of course, there are we parents, who – not surprisingly – don't know what to do. Deciding whether or not to immunize is difficult, and this book won't tell you what to do. I hope that it will, however, answer the crucial questions in your mind, making your decision – if not easier – at least better informed.

Anne Charlish, Sussex, 1996

Part One: The Issues

What is Immunization?

Immunization is the process of inducing immunity as a preventive measure against certain infectious diseases. The terms 'immunization' and 'vaccination' are used interchangeably.

The purpose of immunization is not only to protect individuals but also to eliminate gradually a particular disease from the world.

As a result of immunization, one disease – smallpox – has been completely eliminated, while the incidence of many diseases – such as diphtheria, polio and whooping cough – has declined dramatically, to the point where they are now rare. Others still – such as measles and meningitis – are in steady decline.

It was not until the twentieth century that scientists developed an understanding of immunology that permitted them to immunize people against a wide range of diseases that might otherwise be both common and fatal. These diseases include:

- cholera
- diphtheria
- hepatitis

- measles
- polio
- rubella
- tetanus
- tuberculosis
- typhoid
- whooping cough
- yellow fever

Attempts to develop a vaccine against leprosy and syphilis have so far failed, as have more recent attempts, still actively continuing, to find a vaccine against AIDS.

The news is not all bad though. A new vaccine is being developed that could end all allergic reactions, from mild hay fever to the most severe food allergies, which can have fatal consequences. Human trials are at an early stage, but the vaccine is expected to come onto the market as a prescription drug around 1998.

The History of Vaccination

The technique of vaccination was pioneered in England in the late eighteenth century by Sir Edward Jenner. He noticed that milkmaids who had been exposed to cowpox were immune to the much more dangerous but similar disease, smallpox. No one understood how or why this should be, but the term 'vaccination' was coined in order to describe it for the simple reason that the medical name for cowpox is 'vaccinia'.

Smallpox was once a widespread disease. There were

two strains of smallpox, both of them fatal, though one more deadly than the other. These were variola major and variola minor.

Variola major killed up to 50 per cent of its victims, while variola minor had a death rate of about one in every 200 people who were infected. It caused fever, headache, nausea and aching muscles. Pus-filled blisters covered the face, arms and chest of victims and, if the sufferer survived, they left disfiguring scars.

Today, smallpox has been completely eliminated throughout the world, thanks to an intensive international vaccination campaign organized by the World Health Organization (WHO), which began in 1967. The last reported case of smallpox was a 23-year-old Somalian and, in October 1979, the WHO officially declared that smallpox had been eradicated.

How Immunization Works

Some infectious diseases will occur only once in a person's life. This is because the body's immune system retains a memory of the disease and is therefore ready to fight off any subsequent infection by the same organism. How long this immunity lasts varies. Immunization is simply the process of artificially inducing immunity to diseases.

Types of Immunization

There are two main types of immunization. These are active immunization and passive immunization.

Active Immunization

With active immunization, an altered, or killed, non-infectious form of the disease is administered. This stimulates the immune system to produce antibodies and to 'remember' the organism in the same way it would remember a true infection. If the child is then exposed to the same organism, the immune system produces antibodies in large numbers, which stop the infection.

Passive Immunization

In passive immunization, antibodies are used that have been produced by those who have recovered from a particular infection. Blood is taken from a number of people who have recently recovered from the disease, as their blood contains antibodies against that particular disease organism. Serum containing the antibodies is extracted, pooled with other extracted immune serum, purified and injected into the child who is being immunized. The antibodies immediately attack the disease organism if it is already present, or they provide protection against the organism should it enter the body.

Passive immunization provides immediate but only temporary protection.

What is a Vaccine?

A vaccine is a cocktail of chemicals, which is injected into the bloodstream. It contains protein, bacterial and viral particles, as well as preservatives, neutralizers and carrying agents.

Types of Vaccine

There are three different forms of vaccine which are used nowadays. The first of these is an inactivated vaccine, made of organisms that have been killed or inactivated by heat or chemicals. The vaccine is then purified. Vaccines of this kind are used against:

- whooping cough
- cholera
- typhoid
- influenza

The second type is a weakened, or attenuated, vaccine, which consists of live organisms that have been altered so that they no longer cause infection. Although they are in themselves harmless, the organisms in the vaccine can nevertheless induce immunity. This type of vaccine generally provides the most effective, long-lasting immunity. Vaccines of this kind are used against:

- polio
- measles
- mumps
- rubella
- yellow fever
- hepatitis

The third type of vaccine is derived from an inactivated toxin that has been produced by a disease-causing organism. This type of vaccine is used when the symptoms of the disease are caused by the body's response to the toxin. Vaccines against this type of disease contain modified toxins, called toxoids, which are able to stimulate the production of antibodies, but do not produce illness. Vaccines of this kind are used against:

- tetanus
- diphtheria

How Immunizations are Given

Most immunizations are given by injection, usually into the tissue under the skin or into the muscle. The most common site for this is the outer, upper part of the arm. If the immunization involves a large volume of fluid, it will be injected into the buttock.

Where it is necessary to give mass immunization – as, for example, to military personnel – a special compressed air gun is used, which releases vaccine at such a high pressure that the liquid punctures the skin. This permits many people to be vaccinated in rapid succession.

The polio vaccine is an exception, and is usually given orally, either on a sugar lump or in drops applied to the tongue.

Adverse Reactions

There are usually no after-effects following immunization, although some vaccines cause some pain and swelling at the site of the injection. A few people may also experience a slight rise in temperature along with feelings of irritability and flu-like symptoms. If a child develops a fever after being immunized, he or she should be given paracetamol.

In very rare instances, the reaction to an immunization may be severe. Reactions such as seizures have led to controversy about the safety of certain immunizations, in particular that against whooping cough. The official view in Britain is that the risks of immunization are generally much lower than the risks of the disease itself, although not everyone agrees with this.

One of the most worrying developments was a report on immunization in 1993 by the Institute of Medicine in the USA. This held that virtually all immunizations that are given to children have at some time been proven to cause damage. After their child has been immunized parents assume that everything must be all right if their child does not have a violent reaction such as shock, convulsions or paralysis, but less devastating and longer-term effects may not be so obvious. They can be just as serious, although they may not become evident for many years (*see page 17*).

People who Should Not Be Immunized

There are certain people who should not be immunized. These include:

- sufferers from an immunodeficiency disorder such as AIDS
- cancer patients
- anyone taking corticosteroid drugs

- anyone who has previously had a severe reaction to the same vaccine
- a child who has had a previous severe allergic reaction after eating eggs (a severe reaction means a swollen mouth and throat, difficulty in breathing, shock, or a rash on the face and body)
- anyone suffering from a fever or an infection, in which case vaccination should be delayed
- pregnant women or those planning to get pregnant – your doctor should be consulted as certain vaccines should not be given to you

In addition to this, if a child is suffering from any acute illness, immunization should be postponed until the child is well. Minor infections without fever or systemic upset should not have any effect on immunization. Other than these general guidelines, contraindications are given where appropriate under each specific disease immunization in Part Two.

The Immunization Debate

There can be few subjects that provoke such frenzied, almost hysterical, reactions both for and against as immunization. Any debate on this subject sparks the kind of emotional fervour expressed by religious fundamentalists, not by informed and sensible people taking part in a balanced, scientific debate.

One of the reasons for this is that many of the stories that people have to tell about immunizations are heartbreaking tales of injury and death, of immense harm done to young children, often as young as one or two years old. Stories of little children suffering are, naturally, very emotive.

It is against this background that parents have to steel themselves to make important decisions. Every parent will ask themselves the question: to immunize or not to immunize? So much knowledge seems to be required for even a partial understanding of the complex issues involved that it is difficult to find the right answer.

Immunization Laws

In many countries, including Italy and the USA, immunization against certain diseases is a requirement for entry into school, though parents can opt out in most states on ideological or religious grounds. This is monitored in the US by the Advisory Committee on Immunization Practices and the American Academy of Pediatrics. As a result of this, diphtheria, polio, measles and whooping cough have become rare.

In other countries, such as Britain, immunization is not required by law, but it is performed routinely as part of a childhood immunization programme. The Department of Health recommends immunization, which is monitored by the local health authority.

The Parents' Decision

With all the controversy currently surrounding immunization, the decision of whether or not to have your child immunized is a difficult one, and one not to be taken lightly. Before you can make a decision, you need to ask yourself the following questions:

- Why should you immunize your child?
- Does the immunization give full protection against the disease in question?
- Is it safe?
- Are there any contraindications to your child being immunized?

- Are there any possible adverse reactions to immunization?
- Can protection justify the risks of any adverse reactions?
- Are there any alternatives to immunization?

You can always postpone the decision to immunize until you are sure you have made the right choice. If you do decide to immunize, you won't be able to reverse the effects, so take your time in reaching a decision.

Why Immunize?

A small number of children who contract an acute, contagious illness, such as measles or whooping cough, will develop serious complications. In a very small minority, these can cause such severe reactions as brain damage or even death.

When a child contracts such a disease, he or she usually develops a defensive response which confers immunity for life. The purpose of immunization is to stimulate this defence mechanism artificially whilst eliminating the risk of the disease.

With vaccination, the disease enters the body via the bloodstream and not via the nasal passages as it would if the child caught the disease naturally. Opponents to immunization will argue that, by bypassing the body's defence system, immunization can compromise the immune system and thus the child's overall physical health.

Is Immunization Effective?

The official view is that, although no vaccine provides 100-per-cent guaranteed protection against infection, it works in most cases. In those cases where an individual contracts an infection in spite of immunization, the disease will probably be less severe than it might otherwise have been. No fully immunized child, for example, has ever died from whooping cough.

The incidence of most of the acute, contagious diseases has been reduced in those communities where routine immunization programmes have been carried out. For example, diphtheria has declined in incidence in most European countries. There has, however, also been a reduction of the disease in countries where there is no compulsory immunization. Better hygiene and sanitation have played a crucial part in the battle against the disease.

As Brian Inglis, medical historian, puts it:

> The chief credit for the conquest of the destructive epidemics ... ought to have been given to the social reformers who had campaigned for purer water, better sewage disposal and improved living standards. It had been their efforts, rather than the achievement of the medical scientists, which had been chiefly responsible for the reduction in mortality from infectious disease.

Yet immunization is not always successful. In Britain over 30,000 cases of diphtheria have been recorded in fully immunized children. Similarly, when smallpox was still active, there were also significant numbers of cases of the disease in people who had been vaccinated.

Writing in the *British Medical Journal* in 1928, Dr L. Parry questions the immunization statistics which revealed a higher death rate among those vaccinated against smallpox than the unvaccinated. He asks the following questions:

- How is it that smallpox is five times as likely to be fatal in the vaccinated as in the unvaccinated?
- How is it that in some of our best vaccinated towns, such as Bombay and Calcutta – smallpox is rife, whilst in some of our worst vaccinated towns, such as Leicester, it is almost unknown?
- How is it that something like 80 per cent of the cases admitted into the Metropolitan Asylums Board smallpox hospitals have been vaccinated, whilst only 20 per cent have not been vaccinated?
- How is it that in Germany, the best vaccinated country in the world, there are more deaths in proportion to the population than in England – for example, in 1919, 28 deaths in England, 707 in Germany; in 1920, 30 deaths in England, 354 in Germany. In Germany in 1919 there were 5,012 cases of smallpox with 707 deaths; in England in 1925 there were 5,363 cases of smallpox with 6 deaths. What is the explanation?

Similar doubts have been expressed concerning the statistics of measles and whooping cough. Following closer examination of the statistics, many doctors have also voiced doubts as to the real value of immunization, and have questioned whether it is primarily responsible for the reduction in the number of cases. Diseases such as smallpox and polio, which have now been virtually eradicated, reputedly as a result of vaccination programmes, were already in decline when immunization was introduced. In some cases, only 10 per cent of the population had been vaccinated, and it is therefore more likely that other factors are responsible for the decline in incidence of these diseases.

The incidence of measles also declined before immunization became widespread. At the turn of the twentieth century in England and Wales, the mortality rate for those afflicted with measles was in the region of 318 per million people. By 1956, which was just seven years before immunization against measles began, this figure had declined to less than one per million people. So the statistics do not appear to support the theory.

The eradication of diseases such as smallpox is not necessarily down to better standards of health and immunization. It is suggested that there is merely a changing pattern of disease with other, often more resistant, viral strains taking over. Many viral strains will exist quite harmlessly inside the human body, only to multiply when the conditions are right for them.

How Safe is Immunization?

This is the question that causes parents so much agonizing. The conventional view is that the benefits of immunization outweigh the small risk of side-effects. However, statistical evidence suggesting that the risks of immunization are significantly less than those of the complications of the disease itself are thought to be misleading by some doctors, naturopaths and other health professionals. Such figures take into account only the short-term and immediately observable effects of immunization. Increasingly, however, concern is being expressed about the possible long-term effects.

Although vaccines are designed to stimulate protection against specific viruses, they may make demands on the immune system – especially on the immature defences of young infants – that are far in excess of that of the natural defensive response to the disease itself. A number of eminent medical paediatricians have expressed the view that this may weaken the defences against other viral illnesses, and that there may be a link between childhood immunizations and subsequent diseases later in life, such as cancer, multiple sclerosis, arthritis, allergies, eczema, encephalitis, severe fatigue states and immune deficiency problems such as leukaemia and even AIDS. Yet since this effect is often delayed, indirect and masked, the true extent of long-term damage is difficult to monitor.

Viral elements that are injected directly into a child's bloodstream may persist in the system, and may occasionally mutate, only to emerge many years later. Both the measles and rubella immunizations, for example, have now been identified as being responsible for causing rheumatoid arthritis in young people.

A causal link has even been suggested between mass immunization and an increase in violent crime. One explanation for this is that the thymus, which plays an important role in the immune system, is badly damaged by vaccination. This appears to have an important link with violent behaviour, as a large number of violent criminals have been found to have thymus glands which have not atrophied as they should have done at puberty. More recently, a link has been made between the Mumps, Measles, Rubella (MMR) vaccine and Crohn's disease, which is a debilitating disorder of the bowel.

Damage to a child's immune system is probably the greatest charge that has been laid at the door of the advocates of immunization. In their book, *Vaccinations and Immune Malfunctions*, Doctors Buttram and Hoffman warned of the 'probability of widespread and unrecognized vaccine-induced immune system malfunction and the need for scientific investigation of these effects'.

No scientific studies have, as yet, been carried out to investigate specifically the long-term side-effects of immunization on a person's health. On the whole, most doctors support immunization. Parents are inevitably swayed by this – if all the doctors have faith in it, then it must be for the best.

Opponents to immunization, however, argue that there are three reasons that most doctors continue to support vaccination campaigns. The first is that they are unaware of the evidence against immunization. They don't question what they are told. They simply accept what they were taught in medical school.

The second reason is that they are unwilling to speak out. Even those doctors who are aware of the drawbacks are frightened of being ridiculed, of being disciplined, of losing their position.

And the third reason is that doctors are forced, by Department of Health regulations, to immunize children because of the way in which they are paid. Doctors must vaccinate at least 90 per cent of the children on their register against diseases such as whooping cough, diphtheria, polio, tetanus, measles, mumps and rubella in order to qualify for their annual allowance of £2,000. Failure to meet targets means they are financially penalized. Thus immunization is not exactly obligatory, but it might as well be.

One doctor who didn't allow fear to prevent him from speaking out was Dr Anthony Morris, a well-respected research virologist who worked for the Food and Drug Administration's (FDA) division of biological standards in the USA. In 1976; Dr Morris was dismissed from his post for publicly speaking out against the vaccination programme for swine flu that President Gerald Ford wanted 'every man, woman and child' to receive. Mr Morris called the programme a 'senseless fiasco', and warned that the vaccine was not only ineffectual but could have disastrous consequences. In the event, it caused 41 deaths and over 500 cases of Guillain-Barré Syndrome. Dr Morris believes he was sacked not for wasteful research, as stated by the FDA, but for economic reasons – 'the influenza vaccines were the biggest sellers at the time'.

Dr Morris continues to speak out against immunization in unequivocal terms. 'There is a great deal of evidence to prove that immunization of children does more harm than good,' and 'There is no rationale for forcing immunization,' he claims, but this does not make it any easier for parents to reach their decision. What he says certainly raises doubts, but it doesn't provide all the answers.

What Can Parents Do?

The decision as to whether or not to have your child immunized lies in your hands, once you have familiarized yourself with all the facts. Information on the dangers of the disease itself is readily available from Department of Health leaflets and advertising campaigns. Ask your doctor or complementary practitioner, if you have one, for all the current, up-to-date information available on the risks of vaccination for the particular disease which you are concerned about. The safety record of some vaccinations is better than others, but all carry some risks.

You have the freedom of choice in healthcare for your children, and any reasonable family doctor should respect your wish to decline immunization if you are in any doubt about its suitability for your child.

Are There Alternatives to Immunization?

According to many experts, in particular naturopaths and complementary therapists, the best foundation for your child's immune system is breastfeeding, a healthy diet and a healthy lifestyle, including natural treatment for all minor ailments and the avoidance of chemical additives and refined products. Their argument is that a child who is raised in this way is less susceptible to disease, and – should it occur – will be better equipped to deal with it rapidly and effectively. The childhood contagions will still occur, but some natural immunity will have been conferred and the probability is that naturally reared and treated children are at less risk of complications than those brought up in poor social circumstances with frequent recourse to junk food and synthetic medication.

There are a number of homoeopathic remedies that can be used to treat childhood illnesses. A qualified homoeopath can also help antidote the side-effects of immunization. If you decide against immunization, professional constitutional homoeopathic treatment should be given to boost your child's natural immunity. Protection against childhood illnesses can be given in the form of a homoeopathic prophylactic known as a nosode.

It is worth noting, however, that even practitioners of homoeopathy are not themselves in complete agreement about the benefits of homoeopathic vaccines, and there is no evidence that they provide long-term immunity. The Faculty of Homoeopaths, which is made up of medically qualified homoeopaths, recommends that:

> where there is no medical contraindication, immunization should be carried out in the normal way using conventional tested and approved vaccines … We do not have the research data showing the persistence of satisfactory antibody levels after using homoeopathic preparations for immunization, and this is why the advice is to use the 'conventional' vaccines if at all possible.

Even Samuel Hahnemann, nineteenth-century German physician and founder of homoeopathy, was a strong supporter of immunization, which he considered to be a convincing demonstration of the principle at the basis of homoeopathy that 'like cures like'.

If you decide to opt for orthodox immunization, your child will be treated as shown in the following schedule (© Health Education Authority).

Childhood immunization programme

Age	Immunization	Method
2 months	Haemophilus Influenzae Type b (Hib)	Injection
	Diphtheria, Whooping Cough, Tetanus (DPT)	Injection
	Polio	By Mouth
3 months	Haemophilus Influenzae Type b (Hib)	Injection
	Diphtheria, Whooping Cough, Tetanus (DPT)	Injection
	Polio	By Mouth
4 months	Haemophilus Influenzae Type b (Hib)	Injection
	Diphtheria, Whooping Cough, Tetanus (DPT)	Injection
	Polio	By Mouth

12–15 months	Measles, Mumps, Rubella (MMR)	Injection
3–5 years (around school entry)	Diphtheria, Tetanus	Booster Injection
	Polio	Booster by Mouth
13 years	Tuberculosis (BCG)	Injection
15–19 years (school leavers)	Diphtheria, Tetanus	Injection
	Polio	Booster by Mouth

Government Targets

A row has recently broken out concerning government targets. Eight families belonging to a GP's practice in Presteigne, Powys, Wales, have refused to have their children immunized because of their fears of side-effects, and the doctor has decided to remove them from his practice list. The families put the doctor below the 90 per cent immunization target (*see pages 18–19*), hence his decision to strike them off.

Although immunization may not be an obligatory requirement for children to be admitted to school in Britain, as is the case in the USA and Italy, this regulation seems to be a roundabout way of making immunization compulsory all the same. For some, this is an added pressure and does not help make a parent's decision any easier

Part Two:
Diseases and Immunization

Children are susceptible to a whole range of diseases that are very common in the early years of their lives. What follows is a description of each of these diseases, together with their incidence, causes, signs and symptoms, diagnosis, treatment and possible complications.

The possibility of immunization is discussed in each case, together with contraindications and an assessment of the risks and benefits of immunization as opposed to those of the disease itself.

Chickenpox

Chickenpox, sometimes called varicella, is an infectious disease caused by the varicella-zoster virus, one of the viruses of the herpes group. It is one of the most common and troublesome viruses.

When the infection has cleared up, the virus lies dormant in the dorsal root ganglia, from where it may be reactivated, particularly in elderly people or in people whose immune systems are compromised. If the infection is reactivated, it will reappear as shingles, or herpes zoster, which is a more severe illness and can be very difficult to shake off completely. Doctors do not fully understand exactly what reactivates a virus.

Chickenpox is not usually a dangerous disease and rarely causes complications in children. An attack of chickenpox usually confers immunity to the disease for life.

Incidence

Chickenpox occurs in most countries, and most people throughout the world will have had chickenpox at some point during their childhood, usually by the age of 10. In fact, many parents encourage their children to contract chickenpox while they are young and may even intentionally expose them to other children who have chickenpox, in the hope that they will catch it. This is because chickenpox is a much milder disease in children than in adults.

Causes

Chickenpox is spread by the transmission of airborne droplets during coughing or sneezing, and through contact with a sufferer. Susceptible children who come into contact with someone who is suffering from shingles may develop chickenpox. The incubation period is between 14 and 21 days.

Signs and Symptoms

Illness may start with a day of feeling vaguely unwell, with headache, mild fever and slight nausea. In general, the child does not appear to be ill. The most telling symptom is the appearance of a rash. The spots first appear in the mouth, on the palate and in the throat, and leave ulcers that may be painful as well as causing difficulty in swallowing. These spots are followed on the second day by an itchy rash of small, dark-red spots, which are itchy and sometimes painful. After a few days, the spots burst or dry out, and then crust over. Unlike the skin rash of smallpox, the chickenpox rash starts on the body and spreads to the legs, arms, head and face. Rather than all the spots going through their various stages at the same time, they appear in a succession of crops over several days, so that spots can be seen in all their various stages on the same day. The spots are raised swellings, or blisters, about 2–3 mm in diameter, which contain a clear fluid. They are highly infectious. Old spots will crust over and form scabs, while new ones will appear at intervals over the next few days.

The spots will disappear after about 12 days and the patient will continue to be infectious until all the spots have crusted over. The crusts fall off without leaving any scarring, unless they have developed a secondary infection because they have been scratched, in which case they may start to produce yellow pus.

In children under the age of 10, the disease is normally mild and the child will usually recover completely within approximately 10 days. Chickenpox rarely occurs in adults, but when it does, it is a more serious illness than in children, particularly if the sufferer has a blood disorder, or is on long-term steroid therapy. Recovery takes much longer in adults.

Diagnosis

Chickenpox is usually diagnosed simply from a medical examination of the patient.

Treatment

Treatment is not on the whole necessary, with the only home treatment called for being rest and plenty of fluids, which usually leads to a complete recovery. A doctor should be called, however, if the illness is so severe that the fever is very high or there is excessive coughing or vomiting. He or she will usually prescribe antibiotics, which will prevent further infection. If the mouth is affected, the doctor will prescribe a soothing mouthwash. If the eyes are involved, this will also call for medical attention and the doctor will probably prescribe a soothing eyewash.

Skin irritation can be relieved by applying calamine lotion, or by warm boracic baths. Antihistamine tablets may also prove helpful, and paracetamol will help relieve fever and discomfort caused by the spots.

It is important not to pick the spots, as they can scar to form unsightly pock-marks and can lead to secondary bacterial infection. It is a good idea to cut your child's nails very short to prevent scratching, and it might be best for a young child, who does not understand the hazards of scratching the spots, to wear gloves for a few days when the itching is at its worst. The rash should be kept clean and dry.

Children at school spread infections to one another very easily because they are in such close contact. A child who is suffering from chickenpox should be kept away from school until all the spots have completely dried up and formed scabs.

An antiviral drug known as acyclovir is sometimes used for severe cases of generalized disease and pneumonia, which can follow as a complication, but if it is to work it must be used in the early stages of the disease. In an adult patient who is suffering from a particularly severe form of the disease, the doctor may decide to boost the body's resistance by administering an injection of antiserum.

Complications

Complications do not occur very often. Secondary skin infections may cause spots to lead to boils, impetigo or conjunctivitis in the eyes. Rarely, encephalitis, or inflammation of the brain cells, can occur. This is heralded by drowsiness or sleepiness, when it is difficult to wake the child fully, headache, fear of bright lights, and sometimes unconsciousness. If it happens, encephalitis usually comes on a week or so after the infection has cleared up. It is very serious and requires urgent medical attention.

Adults who get chickenpox may develop pneumonia, with breathing difficulties and fever. Chickenpox can be serious in an immunosuppressed patient because the disease can become generalized and develop into a severe form.

It is therefore advisable for adults who have never had chickenpox to avoid it by staying away from children who have the disease. Women in the final stage of pregnancy, in particular, should be careful to avoid it, since it may be serious in pregnancy and can cause a newborn child to develop a severe attack of the disease.

Immunization

Experimental vaccines have been tried but vaccination is as yet not generally available. The use of vaccines has so far been confined to high-risk groups such as children who are receiving treatment for leukaemia.

Diphtheria

Diphtheria is a dangerous, highly infective disease of the upper respiratory tract (and occasionally of the skin). It is an acute bacterial illness, which most commonly affects the nose, larynx or tonsils and causes sore throat and fever. After the initial throat infection, serious complications can arise, such as difficulties in breathing, muscular weakness and heart or respiratory failure, which can prove fatal.

Some sufferers will have a more serious illness than others because the different strains of the organism responsible for diphtheria produce different amounts of toxin, or poison. Also, serious complications are more likely to arise if a patient's immune system is already weak at the time of infection.

Incidence

Until the 1930s, diphtheria was endemic in the Western world and was one of the greatest global causes of childhood death. Since then, mass immunization, combined with compulsory isolation of infected patients, has reduced the incidence of diphtheria considerably in developed countries. In Britain, for example, there were only two recorded cases of the disease in 1978, and it is now a rare disease, with only 13 cases and no deaths notified between 1986 and 1991. In the USA, mass immunization programmes against diphtheria were started in 1922, and as a result, cases of diphtheria have become extremely rare.

The few cases that still occur nowadays in Britain are almost always among immigrants from developing countries. In these countries, the disease is usually caught from a healthy 'carrier' of the disease, who has acquired immunity to the illness after having recovered from a relatively mild form of the infection. The carrier harbours *diphtheria bacilli* in the skin or nose, and then spreads them through the air by droplet transmission or through touch.

When an outbreak occurs in the Western world, it is important that every effort is made to trace and test people with whom the infected person may have been in contact during the incubation period. It is only in doing so that carriers may be identified and treated.

Diphtheria remains a danger in some of the developing countries and, although no longer a problem in the Western world, is a risk for travellers who have not been immunized.

Causes

Diphtheria is caused by the bacillus *Corynebacterium diphtheriae*, which produces a powerful toxin. This may live in the skin or nose of a person who is immune to the disease. During the course of infection, the bacillus may multiply in the throat or skin. It is spread by droplets which are expelled when an infected person coughs or sneezes. The incubation period is between four and six days.

Signs and Symptoms

Symptoms appear after the incubation period of four to six days. The early symptoms depend on the patient's degree of immunity to the disease. In a person who is not immune, *diphtheria bacilli* multiply in the throat, causing a character-istic greyish membrane to appear over the tonsils, and to stick firmly to the site of infection. It may also spread over the palate or downwards to the voice box (larynx) and the windpipe (trachea). This membrane can cause breathing difficulties. There is also a risk of the membrane obstructing the airway, in which case it may cause suffocation and can prove fatal. The lymph nodes in the neck will usually become enlarged, and in severe cases this causes a 'collar' of swelling, sometimes referred to as the 'bull-neck'. If the tonsils are affected, the throat may be sore, and if the larynx is affected, the voice may become unusually husky and the patient may develop a cough. If the nose is affected, there may also be a blood-stained discharge from it.

Other symptoms include an increase in heart rate and body temperature. Infection is sometimes confined to the skin, in which case a few yellow spots or sores will appear, which look a little like the small fluid-filled blisters associ-ated with impetigo.

Diagnosis

A doctor will make a diagnosis from observation of the listed symptoms. A medical examination of the patient will include examining the throat and feeling for swollen glands.

Treatment

In some cases, the patient will not develop any further symptoms and recovery will soon follow. In other instances, the infected person may become a carrier after they have recovered, in which case there is a possibility of passing the infection on to others. In most cases, however, the patient will become very ill, and will require treatment.

The patient will be isolated in a special ward and treated with penicillin or erythromycin drugs, which kill diphtheria organisms in the throat. The drugs do not, however, work against the bacterial toxin in the blood, so, if diphtheria is suspected, an antitoxin, which is derived from the blood of immunized horses, must be given as soon as possible in conjunction with penicillin. If the treatment is started early enough, the patient is usually cured.

In rare cases a patient may develop severe breathing difficulties and it may be necessary to perform an emergency tracheotomy or tracheostomy. This is a surgical procedure which introduces a breathing tube into the windpipe.

The patient should be kept in isolation until no *diphtheria bacilli* can be detected in the nose or throat. This will be ascertained by taking swabs on six consecutive days.

Complications

Serious complications of diphtheria can be caused by a bacterial toxin that is released by the bacterium into the blood. This only occurs in people who are not immune.

The patient may collapse and die within a day or two of developing throat symptoms, though this is rare. A more common effect is for someone who is recovering from infection to develop heart failure or paralysis of the throat, the respiratory muscles or the limbs, which is caused by the breakdown of the fatty sheaths surrounding the nerve fibres, in a process known as demyelination. Myocarditis, which is an inflammation of the muscular wall of the heart, may occur during the second week of infection but leaves no permanent damage. Later complications of this kind can occur up to seven weeks after initial infection of the throat. If a patient survives the disease, recovery will be complete.

Immunization

The DPT vaccine, which is designed to prevent diphtheria, whooping cough and tetanus, is given routinely in the first year of life in three spaced doses, at two, four and six months of age.

Although diphtheria is now very rare in developed countries, it remains necessary to continue immunizing against it because it is possible for carriers to bring the disease from developing countries where the disease is much more common. Experts believe that if large numbers of children were not given immunity through vaccination, then a worldwide epidemic would occur.

If you are travelling to a developing country where diphtheria is still common and are not sure whether or not you were immunized as a child, you should have your immune status checked. Those who are found not to be immune should consider vaccination.

Contraindications

There are no apparent contraindications to diphtheria immunization during the first five years. If, however, a child has had a severe local or general reaction to a preceding dose, further doses should be avoided. If the child is suffering from any acute illness, immunization should be postponed until after recovery.

Risks Versus Benefits

Immunization against diphtheria is considered to be very important by most doctors and governments. It is seen as safe and effective and to be largely responsible for the considerable decline in the incidence of diphtheria this century. The importance of immunization in this respect must therefore not be underestimated. If effective immunization were to be carried out all over the world, then it would be possible to eradicate diphtheria completely.

The risks still have to be weighed against the proven success of this immunization. The risks are outlined in the chapter on Whooping Cough on page 89.

Measles

Measles is a highly contagious disease caused by a potentially dangerous virus. Its medical name is morbilli or rubeola. Measles spreads throughout the body, though it chiefly affects the skin and respiratory tract, causing a fever and a characteristic rash. It is most commonly a childhood disease, though it can occur at any age and is considerably worse in adults. Children under the age of eight months rarely develop the infection because they have acquired passive immunity from their mothers, which protects them for the first few months of life. An attack of measles usually confers lifelong immunity. There are some children who have contracted the disease a second time, though this is rare.

Measles is a notifiable disease in Britain, which means that an outbreak requires notification, in writing, to the Medical Officer of Environmental Health. This means that, if you suspect you or your child has measles, you must report it to your doctor.

Incidence

Until recently measles was very common worldwide and tended to occur in winter epidemics every two years. It is no longer common in developed countries, thanks to widespread immunization programmes. In Britain, where immunization was introduced in 1968, the number of reported cases fell dramatically to around 100,000 a year and the disease now affects about one child in 50. In 1988, a combined vaccine against measles, mumps and rubella (MMR) was introduced, in the hope that this might encourage more parents to vaccinate their children. In the USA, proof of immunization against measles is required by law before a child can attend school, with the result that only a few thousand cases are reported each year.

Measles remains common in developing countries, where it is responsible for more than one million deaths each year. Deaths are more common in children who are already suffering from malnutrition and whose defences against infection are therefore badly affected. These children are susceptible to a rare malignant form of measles in which acute catarrh and general weakness can lead to collapse and even, in severe cases, to death.

The mortality rate from measles, which is as low as one per 1,000 in Britain and the USA, is as high as 20 per cent in some Third World countries.

Causes

The measles virus is spread by airborne droplets of nasal secretions and saliva, which are ejected into the air when an infected person coughs, sneezes or simply speaks. There is an incubation period of between 8 and 14 days. The infection can be transmitted shortly after the beginning of the incubation period and until one week after the onset of symptoms.

Signs and Symptoms

Symptoms begin to appear once the incubation period is over. The illness begins with a general feeling of being unwell and rather tired, with a fever, runny nose, sore, watery eyes, a dry throat and a cough. In some children, these symptoms are so mild that they are hardly noticeable, whereas in others they can be very severe and may be accompanied by croup, diarrhoea and, in the most severe cases, by convulsions. Then, after about three to four days, the temperature often falls and a crop of tiny white spots, like grains of salt, on a slightly reddened base, appears on the inside of the cheeks. These are known as Koplik's spots and indicate the presence of measles. After about four or five days, the temperature may rise again to around 37.7–38.9°C, at which stage the child will probably begin to complain of thirst and a headache, as well as being irritable and restless. It is at this stage that a brownish-pink rash appears, with flat or slightly raised spots about 3–5 mm in diameter. This rash usually starts on the head and neck, particularly behind the ears, and then spreads down the body to cover all of it, though not usually the limbs. Sometimes the spots spread so much that they appear to merge and produce large red blotches, which are slightly darker in colour than the earlier rash. The Koplik's spots disappear as the rash develops. By the sixth day, the rash will begin to fade and, after a week, all the symptoms may have disappeared.

Another possible symptom is that the lymph glands may become enlarged. A child suffering from measles may complain of headaches and be very lethargic. Some children find that they become sensitive to light, which hurts their eyes. Recovery in a child is usually complete within about 10 days, whereas an adult who catches the disease may take up to four weeks to feel completely well again.

Diagnosis

Diagnosis is made by medical examination of the patient and observation of symptoms. The appearance of Koplik's spots followed by a rash are the most significant indicators. Measles can be especially hard to diagnose in a black-skinned child because the rash simply gives black skin a slightly granular appearance.

Treatment

The fever should be treated with plenty of fluids and parac-etamol, and children should be kept in bed and given a light, nourishing diet. Particular care should be taken with very young children to prevent a case of secondary bacter-ial infection. Antibiotics will not help with the treatment of measles but the doctor may prescribe them in order to treat secondary bacterial infections that can occur as complica-tions. There is a choice of four antibiotics which doctors can prescribe to treat secondary infections: penicillin, amoxy-cillin, erythromycin or cotrimoxazone.

If a child with measles complains that the light irritates their eyes, then it is advisable to keep them in a darkened room.

Complications

Complications are rare but they can be very serious, and are more likely to occur in adults. Problems that can arise include chest and ear infections, which tend to occur two or three days after the appearance of the rash, when the temperature may also be elevated. Other problems at this stage of illness are diarrhoea, vomiting and abdominal pain. Another complication is the incidence of febrile convulsions, which are fairly common but not usually serious.

A viral measles pneumonia is quite common but of minor importance, and it is normally completely resolved. Bacterial pneumonia, however, is a serious complication, particularly in small children. It should always be suspected if a child is severely ill with a bad cough and should be treated with antibiotics.

Otitis media is quite common. This is an inflammation of the middle ear and occurs as a result of infection extending up the Eustachian tube, which connects the back of the nose to the middle ear.

If conjunctivitis develops as a complication, this can lead to corneal ulceration and should be taken very seriously as it can lead to blindness. Careful medication is important in order to prevent this.

One serious complication, however, which occurs in about one in 1,000 cases, is encephalitis, or inflammation of the brain cells. This is heralded by drowsiness or sleepiness, when it is difficult to wake the child fully, headache, fear of bright lights, and sometimes unconsciousness. If it happens, encephalitis usually comes on about 7 to 10 days after the appearance of the rash. It may cause seizures or a coma, and can lead to mental retardation or even death. Encephalitis is very serious and requires urgent medical attention.

Another possible complication – this time a very rare one which occurs only in about one in a million cases – is subacute sclerosing pan encephalitis, which is a progressive brain disorder that can develop months or even years after an acute illness.

Measles can be particularly serious and even fatal in those children who have impaired immunity, such as those who are receiving treatment for leukaemia, and those who are infected with the HIV virus which causes AIDS.

Measles is extremely dangerous during pregnancy, as it can cause the death of the foetus in about one-fifth of all cases.

Immunization

Immunization against measles is routinely offered for babies of about 15 months of age. It is now available in a combined vaccine against measles, mumps and rubella (MMR). The vaccine is considered to be safe and effective. It uses a live attenuated vaccine and is effective in around 97 per cent of cases.

Children under the age of one should not be immunized, nor should those who have any special risk factors, such as a fever or an immunodeficiency disorder.

It is now recommended that a booster vaccination is given to 11- or 12-year-olds because infection has been occurring in teenagers who were immunized during infancy.

Contraindications

Apart from any acute infection, these are fever, severe malnutrition and active tuberculosis.

Risks Versus Benefits

There are a few possible side-effects of the measles vaccine but these do not occur in all cases and are usually mild, including a slight fever, the symptoms of a cold, and the appearance of a rash about a week after immunization.

Although the vaccine has the same side-effects as those of measles itself, the risk associated with vaccination is generally considered by many doctors to be much less than the risk of infection, and this was the view put forward by doctors and government officials in 1995 when a massive immunization programme was launched by the Government.

A great measles epidemic was expected to sweep Britain in 1995, and a £20 million national immunization programme was duly organized, during which some seven million children were immunized. This was one of the most ambitious vaccination initiatives that Britain has ever undertaken. The aim was to vaccinate 95 per cent of the seven million schoolchildren aged between 5 and 16 within just one month, in order to prevent the epidemic of measles that was anticipated early in 1995. The difference in this campaign was that its aim was to *prevent* an epidemic – the more usual response is to wait for an outbreak to occur and then to respond to it.

Now not only are there doubts as to whether a measles epidemic was ever really going to happen, but there are claims on behalf of at least 300 children to the effect that they have been permanently damaged as a result of the vaccine, in spite of the fact that Government officials and doctors assured them that the vaccine had no major side-effects. Damage refers to any sort of change in the child's developmental abilities, due to brain impairment. The Department of Health has denied such allegations.

Dr Richard Nicholson, editor of the *Bulletin of Medical Ethics*, called for an independent inquiry because, he claimed, the Government misled millions of parents into having their children vaccinated. It was claimed that the Government overplayed the possibility of an epidemic, while underplaying the dangers of the vaccine. In a letter to *The Times* (Autumn 1995), Richard Nicholson pointed out that if the latest round of measles immunization were to be put forward as a research project, however limited, it would not be granted a licence. It is clear that more research needs to be carried out.

Data collected by the Communicable Disease Surveillance Centre showed that one adverse reaction, thrombocytopenic purpura, which is a serious bleeding disorder, was in fact five times more likely than had previously been thought. Encephalitis and other neurological complications as well as convulsions, paralysis and death have all been found to be serious risks of vaccination.

Doubt as to the safety of the measles immunization remains. In addition, there are doubts as to its efficacy. British mothers have been told that the measles vaccine appears to be working in other parts of the world, yet the USA is apparently suffering from a steady increase in cases of measles in spite of the fact that the vaccine has been used since 1957. The increasing epidemic has been blamed on clusters of unvaccinated children, particularly among poor, non-white populations, but statistics appear to prove otherwise. Of the 1989 statistics from the Center for Disease Control (CDC) in Atlanta, half of the college-aged victims of measles had previously been vaccinated. In addition to this, between 1985 and 1986, 60 per cent of all measles cases occurred in schoolchildren, most of whom had been vaccinated.

Yet another factor in the measles debate is that the real risks of contracting measles seem to have been overplayed. Opponents to the vaccine argue that children often suffer nothing worse than flu when they get measles, and grow up with true immunity to measles for the rest of their lives. This immunity is far from certain with the vaccine which, it is argued by its opponents, gives nothing more than temporary or imperfect immunity. This means that children who have been immunized could, ironically, grow up susceptible to measles, which is far more serious when experienced as an adult.

In May 1995, the pressure group What Doctors Don't Tell You (WDDTY) revealed the British Government's most embarrassing admission – that the MMR vaccine can increase the risk of seizure five-fold. The discovery is deeply embarrassing for a government that was, only in

Autumn 1994, preparing one of the largest immunization programmes ever undertaken and reassuring the public that the measles vaccine was perfectly safe.

Meningitis

Meningitis is an inflammation of the meninges, which are the three thin layers of membrane that cover the brain and spinal cord. Its existence has been recorded since 1892. Meningitis is caused by an infection which can be either viral or bacterial. Bacterial meningitis, as well as being the rarer of the two forms, is also the more serious, and is life-threatening.

Babies receive no passive immunity to meningitis from their mother, which means that they are susceptible to infection from birth, when the disease is at its most dangerous. Infection is not, however, common in newborns.

Incidence

Meningitis tends to occur in epidemics in the winter months, and the fact that there have been a number of localized epidemics in recent years has attracted a lot of attention. It is not known why outbreaks are more common in some years than others.

Bacterial meningitis affects around 2,000 people each year in Britain, most of whom are young children. It sometimes occurs in small clusters and it can also occur in isolated cases. Meningococcal meningitis – also known as cerebrospinal or spotted fever – is the most common form of bacterial meningitis in the world, and often occurs in epidemics. It is therefore a notifiable disease in Britain (*see page 38*).

Haemophilus influenzae type b (Hib) meningitis is the form of bacterial meningitis that occurs most commonly in young children, with the peak incidence between the ages of 6 to 15 months. It used to be thought to be the cause of influenza – which explains its name – though this was subsequently found not to be true. It is estimated that some 60 out of every 100,000 children will contract this Hib type of meningitis. Of these, it is estimated that between 3 and 6 per cent will die, while a further 14 per cent will have long-term problems such as deafness, learning difficulties and cerebral palsy.

Tuberculous meningitis, which is a much less common type of bacterial meningitis, occurs particularly in young children in those areas of the world where there is a high incidence of tuberculosis.

Viral meningitis affects about 500 people each year in Britain, though it is thought that its true incidence may actually be much higher as it is not a notifiable disease. In the USA, it affects more than 10,000 people each year. It tends to occur in clusters during the winter.

Causes

The viral form spreads from person to person through the air in tiny droplets when an infected person coughs, sneezes or simply speaks. It tends to occur in epidemics, often in winter, as do many viral infections. Many of the potentially causative microbes are constantly present in the noses and throats of most people, though they do not, however, go on to develop the disease. A person's natural resistance has to be lowered before the infection can become established. There are several ways in which infection can reach the meninges. It may spread via the bloodstream. Although less likely, it may also be transmitted through cavities in the skull from an infection in the ear or the sinuses, or from an infection following a head injury involving a fracture of the skull.

There are several different types of organism that can cause meningitis. Meningococcal meningitis is caused by the bacteria of the *Neisseria* family, other members of which are responsible for gonorrhoea. Tuberculous meningitis is caused by the bacillus that causes tuberculosis.

Viral meningitis is caused by any one of a number of viruses, among them those that are responsible for glandular fever, mumps and polio.

Signs and Symptoms

The main symptoms of viral meningitis are a raised temperature, severe headache, a stiff neck, nausea and vomiting, and photophobia (intolerance to bright light). The symptoms of viral meningitis are much milder than those of bacterial meningitis. They can be so mild, in fact, that they resemble influenza.

In meningococcal meningitis, the symptoms can develop rapidly, sometimes within the space of a few hours. The sufferer may feel an intense throbbing pain in the back of the head and then begin to shiver and vomit violently. A raised temperature of 38.9°C or even higher is another indicator. He or she may fall to the ground in a convulsion, and may become delirious. An infected person tends to hold his or her neck rigid because any stretching of the inflamed membranes causes painful spasms. They may feel drowsy and eventually lose consciousness. A red skin rash may develop anywhere on the body. The fontanelle of a young child, which is the baby's soft spot on top of its head, may become swollen and taut instead of being slightly sunken as normal. This is due to an increase in pressure of the cerebro-spinal fluid. In tuberculous meningitis, the patient may feel unwell for a much longer time – up to several weeks – before the characteristic symptoms of meningitis eventually develop.

Diagnosis

Meningitis is diagnosed by isolating the causative organism from a small sample of the fluid that surrounds the brain and the spinal cord. This is done by withdrawing some fluid for examination in a procedure known as lumbar puncture. Diagnosis may be confused with that of meningism, which has relatively similar but innocent symptoms due to a form of meningeal irritation that often occurs in association with some chest infections and diseases of the upper respiratory tract.

Treatment

There is no treatment for viral meningitis, other than rest in a darkened room, plenty of fluids and analgesia. It usually clears up within a week or two, generally with no after-effects.

Bacterial meningitis, on the other hand, is a medical emergency, and requires urgent treatment in hospital with large doses of intravenous antibiotic drugs. Since the development of these drugs, the mortality rate has been reduced from between 70 and 80 per cent to only 10 per cent or below.

If treatment is provided promptly, patients usually recover. If, on the other hand, the patient does not receive immediate treatment, chances of recovery are slim, and the patient will probably die – sometimes within a week of the onset of symptoms.

Complications

There is little risk of any complications developing from viral meningitis, though occasionally patients may suffer from convulsions and some mental deterioration. This only happens in very severe cases.

In bacterial meningitis, however, there is a risk of hydrocephalus developing, which is an accumulation of cerebrospinal fluid in the brain, commonly referred to as 'water on the brain'. In a minority of bacterial meningitis cases there may be some brain damage, and as a result some patients may become blind or deaf. The younger the child, the greater the risk of complications, and elderly people are also at risk of being left with residual brain damage or of dying.

Immunization

Immunization against meningitis caused by the bacterium Haemophilus influenzae type b was first licensed in the USA in 1985, and has been given routinely to children in Britain along with their primary immunizations since October 1992. It is now routinely given in both Britain and the USA because it is the most common form of meningitis in children under the age of six. Vaccination is given at the ages of two, four and six months.

Immunization against other strains of meningitis is of limited value because vaccines exist against only some of the organisms that cause the disease. Protection is, in any case, of limited duration.

Immunization may be of value in controlling an epidemic of certain strains of bacterial meningitis, though giving antibiotic drugs to those who have come into contact with meningitis sufferers is thought to be a more effective treatment.

Contraindications

Immunization should be postponed if the child is suffering from any acute illness until recovery is complete. Other than that, there are no special contraindications.

Risks Versus Benefits

The protective powers of the Hib vaccine are in grave doubt. One study in Minnesota showed that, far from protecting children, the original vaccine actually increased their risk of contracting the disease five-fold. Since then a new vaccine has been introduced to counteract former problems but, according to What Doctors Don't Tell You, this vaccine has a less than impressive track record, too, and seems to be still very much in its experimental stages.

Mumps

Mumps is an acute viral illness, mainly caught during childhood. It is a mild illness in childhood but if it is contracted after puberty it may have serious complications. There are, therefore, distinct advantages in contracting the disease early rather than later in life. Steps should only be taken to isolate from the disease if a child is in a poor state of health. The most obvious sign of mumps is inflammation and swelling of one or both of the parotid glands, which are the salivary glands located just inside the angle of the jaw.

One attack of mumps usually confers lifelong immunity to the disease, though reinfection is possible in a minority of cases.

Incidence

Mumps was a common childhood disease until the introduction of widespread routine immunization. In fact, it was probably the most common infectious disease of childhood. In Britain, mumps affected a large proportion of the population, mostly children between the ages of 5 and 10, and most infections were picked up at school. Mumps is not as contagious as measles, however, with the result that it never tended to spread swiftly through a school in the same way. Immunization was routinely offered to all children from 1988. In the USA, many states require proof of immunization against mumps before admission to school. Since the introduction of routine vaccination, the incidence of mumps has dropped markedly over the last 20 years and is now relatively rare.

Causes

The mumps virus is transmitted in airborne droplets, which are released into the air when a sufferer sneezes, coughs or talks.

There is an incubation period of between two and three weeks between infection and the appearance of symptoms. An infected person may spread the infection for about a week before the onset of symptoms and for up to two weeks afterwards.

Signs and Symptoms

Many children who are infected with mumps have no symptoms, or are only slightly unwell with discomfort experienced in the area of the parotid glands. In more serious cases, a child will experience pain in this area and may have trouble opening their mouth, chewing or swallowing food. The glands on one or both sides of the face may then become swollen, giving a child a hamster-like appearance, and may become very painful. The child could also develop a fever and headache, though the temperature will drop after two or three days. The swelling will probably subside within a week to 10 days. If the gland is swollen only on one side, the

second side may then swell just as the swelling on the original side subsides. The usual outcome is complete recovery within around 10 days.

Diagnosis

Diagnosis is usually made from observation of the patient's symptoms. It is possible to confirm the diagnosis by measuring antibodies to the mumps virus in a sample of blood, or by culturing the virus from samples of saliva or urine.

Treatment

Most cases of mumps are fairly mild, although this is not always true. There is no specific treatment for mumps. An affected child will probably be given painkillers and plenty of fluids to drink. In a fairly severe case, the child may need bed rest for the first few days. The child should stay away from school until the symptoms have cleared up.

You should, however, contact your doctor if the salivary glands or the testes are particularly painful. The doctor will probably prescribe an anti-inflammatory steroid drug, which will reduce both pain and swelling.

Complications

Serious complications are rare. In teenage and adult males, however, mumps can be a very uncomfortable illness, causing a painful inflammation of one or both testes (usually only one). This is known as orchitis and develops in about one-quarter of all cases in men who contract mumps after puberty. It usually lasts for about two to four days. After recovery, the affected testis may become much smaller than it was before. If both testes are affected, orchitis can lead to infertility, though this is rare. Severe orchitis can be treated with strong painkillers, and corticosteroid drugs are prescribed to reduce inflammation. Because of the possible complication of orchitis, males who are past the age of puberty and have never had mumps and have not been immunized should avoid contact with anyone infected with mumps.

An occasional complication of mumps is meningitis, which may give rise to fever, drowsiness, headache, unusual sensitivity to light (known as photophobia) and a stiff neck. Mumps meningitis is not usually serious and normally clears up without leaving any lasting effects (*see pages 51–2*).

A much less common complication following infection with mumps is pancreatitis, as the virus can also affect the pancreas. This causes abdominal pain and vomiting, and usually passes within a few days.

Other possible complications which are rare but serious include meningoencephalitis, deafness, facial palsy, arthritis, rheumatic fever and thrombocytopenic purpura, which is a blood disorder characterized by a lack of platelets in the blood.

Immunization

Immunization against mumps is routinely offered for babies of about 15 months of age and is available in a combined vaccine against measles, mumps and rubella (MMR). This is administered by using a live attenuated vaccine and is effective in around 97 per cent of cases.

There are a few possible side-effects of the MMR vaccine but these do not occur in all cases and are usually mild, including a slight fever, the symptoms of a cold, and the appearance of a rash about a week after immunization.

If a male who is past the age of puberty and has never had mumps or been immunized against it develops symptoms of mumps, passive immunization with an immunoglobulin injection may be beneficial in preventing the development of orchitis.

Contraindications

Immunization should be postponed if the child is suffering from any acute illness until fully recovered. Children under the age of one should not be immunized, neither should those who have any special risk factors, such as a fever or an immunodeficiency disorder.

Risks Versus Benefits

According to What Doctors Don't Tell You, there is little justification for mumps to be a component in the MMR vaccine. Dr Norman Begg, consultant epidemiologist of the Public Health Laboratory Service, which recommended the vaccine in Britain, admits that mumps on its own is a very mild disease in children. Mumps, he admits, 'very rarely' causes any long-term complications. Which begs the question, why immunize against it?

It has been reported in *The Lancet* (1991) that the mumps vaccine has induced meningitis in one per million doses. In addition, according to What Doctors Don't Tell You, there are reports that the mumps vaccine has caused encephalitis, seizures and deafness. One German doctor reported in 1989 that his country's authorities had come up with 27 neurological reactions to the mumps vaccine, including meningitis, febrile convulsions, encephalitis and epilepsy.

These risks have to be weighed against the largely benign effects of mumps.

The risks associated with the triple MMR vaccine against measles, mumps and rubella are discussed on pages 44–7.

Polio

Polio is the common name for poliomyelitis, an infectious disease. It usually causes nothing more than a mild illness, but in more serious cases it attacks the brain and spinal cord, which can lead to paralysis of the motor, or muscle-controlling, nerves running from the spinal cord to the muscles. In a very small number of cases, polio can prove to be fatal.

Since the introduction of routine immunization in the 1950s, polio is virtually unheard of in most of the developed countries.

Incidence

Polio was once a common disease, with particularly large epidemics occurring in the 1950s, when approximately 8,000 people developed the paralysing form of the disease each year in Britain. Polio has now virtually been eradicated from Britain since routine immunization was introduced in 1956, and incidence has dropped from several thousand cases a year to fewer than 10, though it can still occur in people who have not been fully vaccinated. Polio remains a risk in certain parts of the world, including southern Europe, Africa and Asia, where the vaccine is not routinely available. Although polio is no longer a problem in Britain, there is still a risk for people who have not been vaccinated who are travelling to other countries. The World

Health Organization (WHO) is campaigning vigorously for polio to be eradicated worldwide by the beginning of the next century.

In countries where hygiene is poor, children often become infected early on in life. The disease rarely causes more than a mild illness and, as a result, children develop immunity. Ironically, in countries where standards of hygiene are better, children do not gain immunity to the disease by earlier exposure, which means that catastrophic epidemics can occur.

In a mild case of the disease, patients suffer no paralysis, but in a more severe form of the illness, paralysis may take over in only a few hours. Of the patients suffering from nonparalytic polio, recovery is usually complete. Of those suffering from paralytic polio, more than half of them eventually make a full recovery, while less than a quarter are left with severe disability and fewer than one in 10 dies. Adults are usually the worst affected, and the extent of the paralysis is thought to depend on the amount of physical exercise taken by the sufferer during the incubation period, in that the more vigorous the exercise, the more extensive the paralysis.

Causes

Polio is caused by a virus. There are, in fact, three closely related polio viruses, all of which can be responsible for the disease. Transmission is by particles of the virus being carried in faeces, which can then be spread via people's fingers to food. It is also possible for the disease to be transmitted by airborne droplets. There is an incubation period of between three and five days.

Signs and Symptoms

Around 85 per cent of children who are infected with the virus develop only a mild form of the disease. These children have no symptoms at all. For those who do have symptoms, illness will probably last for a few days, during which time they experience a slightly raised temperature, sore throat and headache, and may also vomit. Most children go on to recover completely.

In a few children, however, a short period of seemingly good health may be followed by a severe illness, with symptoms caused by an inflammation of the membranes covering the brain and spinal cord, known as the meninges. Symptoms are likely to include fever, a severe headache, pain and stiffness in the neck and back, and general aching in all the muscles of the body, sometimes with associated twitching. In a severe case, muscular weakness may develop in only a few hours to widespread paralysis of the affected muscles. The muscles that are most commonly paralysed are those of the legs and lower trunk. If the infection extends to the lowest part of the brain (known as the brainstem) the effect may be difficulty in swallowing and breathing, or even total loss of these functions.

Diagnosis

The combination of paralysis of the muscles together with an acute feverish illness is usually sufficient for an immediate diagnosis to be made. If there is any doubt, the only way of making a firm diagnosis is by carrying out a lumbar puncture (*see page 51*). Diagnosis is also sometimes made by taking a throat swab or a sample of faeces.

Treatment

There is no suitable drug treatment for polio. People suffering from a mild form of nonparalytic polio do not normally need any treatment, other than bed rest and painkillers.

Someone who is suffering from paralysis, on the other hand, is likely to need physiotherapy, both in order to prevent damage to the muscles while the virus is still active and then to help muscle function return to normal during convalescence. If the patient is suffering from paralysis that makes breathing impossible, it may be necessary to perform an emergency tracheostomy or tracheotomy (*see page 35*). If the lower part of the body has been paralysed, the bladder will not function correctly and it may be necessary to insert a sterile flexible tube, or catheter, into the bladder in order to drain urine.

Complications

Fewer than a quarter of patients suffering from a paralytic form of the disease are left with a permanent disability and a few – around one in 10 – will die, usually from respiratory paralysis. In a few of the patients who suffer from extensive paralysis and have made some degree of recovery, it is possible for a postpolio deterioration to take place years later, with new areas of weakness and pain in some of the muscles that were thought to have recovered.

Immunization

Vaccination is given during infancy, usually at around three, five and nine months, usually at the same time as diphtheria, tetanus and whooping cough, with a booster dose at around five years. The vaccine contains all three types of polio virus and confers immunity to all three.

There are two forms of vaccine that can be given. The first is Inactivated Polio Vaccine (IPV), which contains dead viruses and is administered by injection into the muscle. This used to be the only type of vaccine available. The second, which is the vaccine most often used in Britain and the USA, is Oral Polio Virus Vaccine (OPV), which contains live but harmless strains of the virus and is administered orally, usually on a sugar lump. This type of vaccine is both less expensive to produce and easier to administer. Children who have an immunodeficiency disorder, which lowers resistance to infection, are treated differently and are usually given IPV.

There is a minimal risk – around one in five million cases – of the live vaccine causing polio in the person who has been vaccinated, or in a close contact of that person.

Contraindications

According to Ronald S. Illingworth, Emeritus Professor of Child Health at the University of Sheffield and formerly Paediatrician to the Children's Hospital, Sheffield, in his book *Infections and Immunisation of Your Child* (Churchill Livingstone, 1981), polio immunization should be postponed if the child has diarrhoea or is feverish. He also points out that:

> There is an exceedingly small risk that if the parents or others in the family have not been immunized, they could be infected by the child who has just been immunized; ideally, they should be immunized at the same time.

Risks Versus Benefits

According to What Doctors Don't Tell You, the current polio vaccine is causing the only new cases of polio in the West and several governments, including the USA Government, are currently considering whether or not to replace it. Many parents remember their grandparents' stories about children disabled to such an extent by polio that they were encased in an iron lung. As a result, many of even the most virulent anti-vaccination parents accept that the polio jab is the one exception and that it would be irresponsible not to vaccinate their children against this most dreaded of diseases.

The effectiveness of the polio vaccine has been the subject of some debate, however, and outbreaks of polio have been seen to occur more commonly among immunized than non-immunized populations. According to immunization expert Dr J. Anthony Morris, formerly of the Food and Drug Administration (FDA) and later of the Institute of Health in America, 'Every time we have an outbreak, the FDA blames it on a "subpotent" vaccine. The fact is that many lots of the vaccine used to fail.'

His view is supported by What Doctors Don't Tell You, who point out that, in any case, polio is not the virulent mass-killer it once was. Most cases of polio are now only mild infections. Far from protecting you from polio, the killed virus (IPV) may prevent you from getting the paralysing form of the disease, but may enable the virus to live on in your gut, which may mean that you could, in theory, pass it on to someone else.

As for the live vaccine (OPV), this has an even worse safety record, with a high risk of the recipient getting polio. As a result, several governments, including that of the USA, are considering reverting to the IPV form of the vaccine, and pharmaceuticals companies in both Europe and the USA have developed an enhanced killed vaccine. A still more worrying complication has been found. According to Dr Anthony Morris, the new enhanced killed vaccine and similar agents have been recovered from brain tumours and pre-cancerous conditions in the brain.

So would Dr Morris vaccinate his grandchildren against polio? 'The answer is: only if they were travelling to places like Egypt during the summer months.'

Rubella

Also known as German measles (in spite of the fact that there are few similarities to measles), rubella is a viral infection which normally only causes a mild illness – usually no more inconvenient than a common cold – in children. As with many of the other diseases already discussed, rubella causes a more severe illness in adults. Rubella is particularly dangerous for women in the early stages of pregnancy, when the foetus can become infected, causing a range of birth defects, including deafness, heart disease, certain eye disorders and cerebral palsy (also known as rubella syndrome). An attack of rubella will usually provide lifelong immunity to the disease.

Incidence

Rubella was once a widespread disease across the world, though it was never as common as true measles, probably because it is less contagious and therefore does not tend to occur in epidemics – for instance, spreading through a school – in quite the same way.

Thanks to routine immunization programmes, rubella is no longer as common as it used to be in developed countries. Immunization was targeted at teenage girls and women planning a pregnancy in Britain until 1988, when a combined vaccine against measles, mumps and rubella (MMR) was introduced for small children.

Causes

Rubella is caused by a ribivirus of the family Togaviridae. The rubella virus is transmitted in airborne droplets, which are ejected into the air when an infected person coughs, sneezes or speaks. The incubation period is between two and three weeks.

The exception to the usual method of transmission is when the virus is transmitted by a pregnant woman to her baby.

Signs and Symptoms

Infection is most common in unimmunized children between the ages of 6 and 12. In most cases, the illness is nearly always mild and it may even pass unnoticed. The first sign of infection is usually a rash, which takes the form of small pink spots about 2–3 mm in diameter, which remain distinct units and do not run together as in true measles. The spots appear first of all on the forehead and face, and then spread to the trunk and limbs. Sufferers will often experience a sore throat and mild conjunctivitis, and unlike true measles, there are no Koplik's spots in the mouth. There may also be a slightly raised temperature and enlarged lymph nodes at the back of the neck, which may be tender, though there are rarely any symptoms of feeling unwell. The rash usually lasts for a few days, before disappearing. By the fourth or fifth day, all symptoms have usually faded away.

In older children and adults who contract the infection,

symptoms are likely to be more severe, with a headache and a more marked fever. A person is infectious from a few days before the appearance of symptoms until one day after they disappear.

Diagnosis

Rubella may sometimes be confused with other viral infections and with scarlet fever, making diagnosis difficult. It can only be positively diagnosed by laboratory isolation of the virus from a throat swab, or by blood tests for antibodies to the virus.

Treatment

There is no effective treatment for rubella. Home treatment usually includes bed rest, though this may not be necessary depending on how unwell the patient feels; plenty of fluids to drink; and paracetamol to reduce the temperature.

Complications

A possible, though rare, complication of infection is polyarthritis, which is a mild and transient form of arthritis causing inflammation of several joints. This usually occurs after the rash has faded and lasts for only a short time. This complication mainly affects adults suffering from the disease.

Encephalitis, or inflammation of the brain cells, is another possible complication, though this is rare and occurs in only about one case in 6,000. Encephalitis may cause seizures and a coma, and can lead to mental retardation or even death. Encephalitis is a very serious condition and requires urgent medical attention.

The most serious complication of rubella is when a pregnant woman is infected during the first four months of her pregnancy, when she is likely to pass the illness on to the foetus. If the illness is caught very early on in pregnancy, this may result in miscarriage. If miscarriage does not occur but the baby is infected, it may be born with one or several congenital defects. The earlier rubella is contracted in pregnancy, the more likely the baby is to be affected. When infection occurs during the first four weeks of pregnancy, for example, more than 50 per cent of babies are likely to be born with a major defect. By the thirteenth week, that figure has dropped dramatically to as few as 8 per cent and continues to decrease steadily from then on.

The type of defect also depends on the state at which the mother is in contact with the rubella carrier. The earlier it happens, the more serious the defect. Congenital abnormalities include, in order of frequency: deafness, congenital heart disease, mental impairment, cataract and other eye disorders, purpura, cerebral palsy, and bone abnormalities. In around 20 per cent of cases, the baby will die in early infancy. There is also an increased incidence of stillbirth. A baby who has contracted the disease is likely to continue to harbour the virus and may spread the infection through saliva, urine and faeces for up to a year after birth.

Foetal injury is not absolutely inevitable. A proportion of women who have had rubella in the early stages of pregnancy go on to produce live, healthy babies. There is, however, a very real risk to the baby and rubella should always be taken seriously.

Immunization

The rubella vaccine is given in a combined form with triple vaccines against measles, mumps and rubella (MMR) when infants are about 15 months old. Reactions to the vaccine are usually negligible.

Any woman of childbearing age who is likely to become pregnant and is not sure whether or not she is immune to rubella, either because she has been immunized or because she has previously had rubella, should have an immune status check. If she is not immune, she should seriously consider immunization. The vaccine should not be given to patients with Hodgkin's disease or leukaemia, or to those on immunosuppressive therapy.

A pregnant woman who is not immune should not be vaccinated because of the risk of damage to the foetus. She should avoid contact with anyone who has rubella and if, in spite of all her efforts, she does make contact with a rubella sufferer, she should seek her doctor's advice immediately. It may be possible to administer passive immunization by injection of immunoglobulin, which may help prevent infection of the foetus.

Contraindications

An infant should not be immunized if an acute illness or a high temperature is present. In addition to this, a woman should not be immunized if she is pregnant, and pregnancy should be avoided for one month after immunization.

Risks Versus Benefits

The official view is that reactions to the rubella vaccine are, according to both the Government and many doctors, minimal. Although the disease itself is unlikely to be severe or even particularly unpleasant, the risks to an unborn child are such that the advantages of routine immunization are believed to be considerable.

As rubella is such a mild illness in children and rarely leads to any long-term complications, you may ask why immunize against it? The risks of the MMR vaccine, as described in the section on Measles on pages 44–7, are not in dispute. In addition to these, the rubella component of the vaccine is known to cause long- or short-term arthritis in 3 per cent of children and between 12 and 20 per cent of adult women. According to Wellcome's Datasheet Compendium, 'symptoms [of arthritis] may persist for a matter of months, or, on rare occasions, for years.' These risks have to be weighed against the largely mild effects of rubella.

What, however, of the main aim of protecting women from developing rubella when they are pregnant, which could otherwise result in serious birth defects? According to What Doctors Don't Tell You, the rubella vaccine has a high failure rate and provides imperfect immunity which can last for as short a time as five years. The purpose of the vaccine was to eliminate the disease in children of both sexes and thus to reduce the risk to adult women. If the vaccine becomes ineffective, which appears to be the case, women who have never had the disease will be at much greater risk of catching rubella when they are pregnant. Catching rubella as a child is relatively harmless and would create a natural immunity which usually lasts for life.

Tetanus

Tetanus is a serious disease of the central nervous system and is commonly known as lockjaw because of the characteristic stiffness of the jaw that it may cause. The stiffness can be so bad that it is difficult, if not impossible, for the mouth to be opened. Tetanus is caused by bacterial infection of a wound, and can sometimes prove fatal.

Incidence

Approximately half a million cases of tetanus occur annually across the world. In Britain, there are fewer than 20 reported cases each year. Between 1985 and 1991, for example, there were 104 cases of tetanus in Britain, resulting in 19 deaths. The low incidence rate of tetanus in Britain is largely due to the routine immunization programme which was introduced nationally in 1961 (the armed forces were immunized from 1938 and some regions from the mid–50s). The cases that still occur in Britain are amongst the non-immunized, mostly people over the age of 50. Overall mortality among people with the disease is about 10 per cent.

In developing countries, where routine immunization does not take place, it is common for newborn babies to die of tetanus as a result of the umbilical stump becoming infected by spores.

Causes

Tetanus occurs if a wound is infected by spores of the bacterium *Clostridium tetani*, which is a normal inhabitant of the alimentary tract of horses and sheep. As a result of faecal contamination, the spores live principally in soil and manure and are particularly prevalent on cultivated land, but can be found elsewhere, such as in the human intestine.

If the spores enter a wound and infect tissues of the body that are badly supplied with oxygenated blood, they multiply and produce a powerful toxin which travels along the motor nerves that control muscle activity to the central nervous system. The affected wound is likely to be a deep one, but an insignificant wound which appears to have healed can also lead to tetanus.

The incubation period is variable – usually between one day and two weeks – and has an important bearing on prognosis. If tetanus appears within only a few days of a wound, it is usually fatal. On the other hand, if symptoms do not appear for two or more weeks after the wound, the disease will probably be mild.

Signs and Symptoms

The most common symptom of tetanus is stiffness of the jaw (trismus). The jaw can become so stiff that it is difficult to open the mouth. Other possible symptoms include stiffness of the muscles of the abdomen and back, which may become as rigid as a board, and a contraction of the facial muscles which causes a strange, fixed, humourless smile, known to doctors as *risus sardonicus*. The patient may also have a slightly quickened heart rate, a slightly raised temperature, and profuse sweating. Painful muscle spasms may develop which, if they affect the larynx or the wall of the chest, may cause asphyxia and can result in death. If the spasm phase of the disease starts within just a couple of days of the appearance of trismus, this indicates a severe case of tetanus. If, on the other hand, there is a long delay before the onset of spasms, the prognosis is more promising. The patient will experience less stiffness, and be able to arch the back, stretch the legs and clench the teeth. A spasm may last for only a few seconds, or continue for several minutes. In severe cases, spasms may interfere with swallowing and breathing. Muscle spasms usually disappear in 10 to 14 days.

Diagnosis

Diagnosis of tetanus is often difficult until the spasms start, since the bacteria are rarely found in the wound. Diagnosis is usually by observing the patient's symptoms, but, because of the difficulty associated with diagnosis, treatment tends to be given routinely to anyone who has an unclean wound, especially if the person concerned is in a high-risk occupation.

Treatment

The wound is thoroughly cleaned and, if necessary, drained of pus. A course of tetanus antitoxin injections is usually necessary. The chosen antitoxin is usually tetanus immunoglobulin. A course of intravenous antibiotics is also given in order to eradicate the organism. A patient suffering from a severe form of the disease should be given 24-hour nursing care in order to keep an eye on muscular spasms. The patient is usually nursed in a quiet, specially darkened room and the bed clothes may be supported by a metal cage. The patient must be handled gently, as any sudden noise, light or pressure may trigger off spasms. Spasms can be controlled by a tranquillizer such as diazepam, or a muscle relaxant. As long as treatment is given promptly, recovery is usually complete.

Complications

If the patient is having trouble breathing, it may be necessary to perform an emergency trachoetomy (*see page 35*) and to administer artificial ventilation.

Immunization

In Britain, the triple DPT vaccine, for diphtheria, pertussis (whooping cough) and tetanus, is given routinely to babies in the first year of life, in three spaced doses, at two, four and six months of age. It is then recommended that tetanus booster shots be given every 10 years. Booster shots are particularly important for people at the greatest risk of infection, such as farmers, veterinary surgeons and gardeners. People should keep their own records of dates of booster shots, as some people may react badly to these injections if they are given too soon.

Contraindications

The tetanus vaccine should not be given to someone suffering from an acute febrile illness, unless the wound is likely to give rise to tetanus.

Risks Versus Benefits

The official view on tetanus is that the benefits of taking a vaccine far outweigh the risks. Yet the degree of effectiveness of the tetanus part of the triple DPT vaccine has been shown to vary considerably from one preparation to another. According to What Doctors Don't Tell You, the vaccine has been purified and made safer precisely in order to prevent reactions to it, and its protective ability has declined proportionately. In spite of this, and again according to WDDTY, the tetanus vaccine can still cause high fever, pain, nerve damage to the inner ear, and degeneration of the nervous system. WDDTY quotes the *New England Journal of Medicine* as reporting, in 1981, that tetanus boosters can cause T-lymphocyte blood count ratios to plunge temporarily to below normal levels – similar to those found in sufferers from AIDS.

A few people are allergic to the anti-tetanus serum and react so severely to it that they can develop anaphylactic shock, which provokes the release of massive amounts of histamine and other chemicals that have a serious effect on body tissues, including a sudden lowering of blood pressure and a widening of the blood vessels. Anaphylactic shock is a dangerous, life-threatening allergic reaction and calls for emergency medical help. An injection of adrenaline is often life-saving.

The triple DPT vaccine is discussed in more detail in the section on Whooping Cough, on pages 94–8.

Tuberculosis

Tuberculosis is an infectious bacterial disease, commonly known as TB. It develops slowly and can lead to chronic ill health. If untreated, it can prove fatal.

Incidence

Tuberculosis used to be common worldwide and caused many deaths in childhood and early adulthood. In nineteenth century Europe, it was responsible for about one-quarter of all deaths.

Its incidence has fallen dramatically in developed countries, thanks mainly to large-scale immunization. Tuberculosis does, however, remain a problem throughout the rest of the world. There are estimated to be some 30 million people suffering from active tuberculosis, causing about three million deaths a year, especially in people whose resistance is low because of disease or malnutrition.

The incidence of tuberculosis in Europe and the USA has decreased steadily over the last few decades. Yet this trend has recently seen a reversal in Britain, largely because of the high incidence of TB among immigrants from the Indian subcontinent, who are 25 times more likely to develop TB and who account for more than one-third of all new cases in Britain. There were about 6,000 new cases reported annually in Britain as recently as the late 1980s. In 1994, there were 5,500 cases in England and Wales. London has three times the national average of cases.

Another reason for the reappearance of tuberculosis in Europe and the USA is that it is affecting growing numbers of people with weakened immune systems as a result of HIV infection and AIDS. Yet another explanation for the rise in cases is that, according to the US National TB Center, the bacteria has become resistant to drugs, with the result that more expensive and more toxic drugs now have to be used. It is now a criminal offence in the USA to refuse to take the available drugs if you suffer from TB.

Tuberculosis used to affect mainly young people, in particular young women. Nowadays, however, most sufferers in the developed world are male and over the age of 45. Tuberculosis is more prevalent in deprived city areas, and amongst the elderly. It tends to occur most readily in people who are suffering from immunodeficiency disorders or diabetes mellitus, and in alcoholics. It is also more common in close contacts of a person who is already suffering from tuberculosis and for this reason it is common for relatives and close friends of a tuberculosis sufferer to be traced so that they can be tested for infection.

Cattle are regularly checked in the developed countries for TB. Milk is in any case heat treated, so that cow's milk is no longer a source of infection. This is not, however, the case in developing countries.

Causes

Tuberculosis is caused by three species of bacteria. These are: *Mycobacterium tuberculosis*, which is responsible for most infections in humans; *M. bovis*, which causes the disease in cattle; and an unnamed and variable mycobacterium, which can cause a rare strain of the disease. This is transmitted by airborne droplets, which are ejected into the air when an infected person coughs, sneezes or speaks. The bacteria are then breathed into the lungs, where they multiply to form a primary infection, or an infected 'focus'. In the great majority of cases, the body's own immune system prevents the infection from spreading at this point and most, or all, of the bacteria are either destroyed or walled in by a fibrous capsule that develops around the inflamed area. Healing will then begin, leaving a scar, and the person will have good immunity against further attack.

In a small minority of cases, however – estimated to be around 5 per cent – infection spreads via the lymphatic system to the lymph nodes. Bacteria can enter the bloodstream at this stage and then spread through to other parts of the body, which is known as miliary tuberculosis and can prove fatal.

In other instances, the bacteria go into a dormant state in the lungs and other organs, and may be reactivated later – sometimes after many years – when the person affected is weak, ill or undernourished. In this secondary phase of tuberculosis, sometimes called consumption, progressive damage may occur, such as the creation of cavities in the lungs. Secondary outbreaks of tuberculosis can be stopped if they are adequately treated, but they may leave bad scar tissue in places where previously healthy tissue has been damaged, and this can have a long-term disabling effect.

Occasionally, the primary infection is not in the lungs

but in the lymph nodes in the neck, intestines, brain, bones, kidneys or other organs.

Cattle are also susceptible to a form of the disease. This means that it can be carried in cow's milk and can enter the human body via the intestine or the tonsils.

The incubation period is about three to eight weeks from the time of infection to the development of symptoms.

Signs and Symptoms

In many people the symptoms of a primary infection are vague, flu-like symptoms. If the disease progresses to the secondary stage, tuberculosis usually affects the lungs, so the main symptoms are generally coughing, which may bring up blood and pus-filled sputum, chest pain and shortness of breath. Other indicators include a raised temperature and associated sweating, especially at night, together with a poor appetite and weight loss.

If any other body organ is affected other than the lungs, the symptoms of an infection of that organ will eventually become apparent, but this may only happen gradually.

Diagnosis

Diagnosis is made by considering a patient's symptoms. A chest X-ray will probably be taken and an abnormal X-ray will show areas of opacity that indicate tuberculosis. In particular, the upper parts of the lung may show the effects of tuberculosis, and cavities may be visible. Old areas of tuberculosis that have since healed will often show up as persistent shadows.

Tests on the sputum (phlegm) will be carried out to reveal the presence of the tuberculosis organism. Attempts may also be made to grow the bacteria from the sputum or from other body fluids, though this test can take as long as six weeks to show any results.

A tuberculin test may also be carried out. A positive result shows that a person has either been infected, or has been immunized against tuberculosis.

If there is still any doubt over the diagnosis, a piece of tissue – say from a lymph node – may be removed in a procedure known as bronchoscopy, and examined.

Treatment

Modern antibiotic drugs are very effective against tuberculosis, though it is often necessary to take at least two different drugs in order to avoid bacterial resistance to them. In Britain, it is common for three or four drugs to be prescribed for two months, followed by two further drugs for another six or seven months. About 5 per cent of patients may have an adverse reaction to the drugs, usually in the form of a rash or a fever. Providing that the patient takes the full course of treatment and rests, most patients will recover completely and will suffer no recurrence. You will be given periodic check-ups for at least two years to make sure that the disease does not recur.

It may be considered necessary to take blood tests at

regular intervals during treatment to make sure that the drugs are not exerting a toxic effect on the liver.

Complications

There are two main complications of tuberculosis of the lungs: the collection of fluid between the lung and the chest wall, which is known as pleural effusion; and air between the lung and the chest wall, which is known as pneumothorax.

Infection of the tonsils or digestive tract may cause an abscess in the neck of the abdominal cavity. This is a condition known as tuberculous peritonitis.

The most serious complication of all is death, which occurs in a minority of cases.

Immunization

An important preventive measure against tuberculosis is the use of an attenuated strain of the *tubercle bacillus* (Bacille Calmette-Guerin) or BCG vaccination. In Britain, this is a procedure that is followed with all high-risk groups, including babies that are born into families with a history of tuberculosis, and with children at around the age of 12 or 13.

Complications include abscesses and persistent ulceration at the site of injection, and enlargement of the axillary lymph glands. Antibiotic treatment may be required.

Contraindications

According to Ronald S. Illingworth, Emeritus Professor of Child Health at the University of Sheffield and formerly Paediatrician to the Children's Hospital, Sheffield, in his book *Infections and Immunisation of Your Child* (Churchill Livingstone, 1981), tuberculosis immunization should not be given if the child has eczema or a general skin complaint.

Risks Versus Benefits

The World Health Organization have used BCG vaccination on a large scale in India, Africa and parts of Asia, and few side-effects have been recorded. Declining incidence of TB in Europe and the USA has reduced the value of BCG vaccination, and it may be that it will in future be reserved only for those who are at high risk.

According to What Doctors Don't Tell You, there is strong evidence that neither the BCG vaccine nor the test to check sensitivity actually works. They report a complication rate of the vaccine of between 0.3 and 0.6 per cent, while it would seem that, among those vaccinated, the resulting protection seems to be greater against leprosy than it is against tuberculosis. WDDTY say that there is ample evidence to suggest that the BCG vaccine may cause serious damage to the immune system and that, increasingly, many doctors believe that M.E. (myalgic encephalomyelitis), also known as post-viral fatigue syndrome, could be caused by drugs that interfere with the immune system in this way.

Whooping Cough

Pertussis is a serious infectious disease, more commonly known as whooping cough, which affects the respiratory system. It occurs mainly in infants and young children. The characteristic feature of this disease is a series of very severe bouts of coughing, when air is expelled from the chest, which often ends in the characteristic 'whoop' (from which the disease gets its name), then air is drawn in again. Coughing can last up to several weeks. Whooping cough leads to inflammation of the upper respiratory tract. Babies receive no passive immunity from their mother, which means that they are susceptible to infection from birth, when it is at its most dangerous. It is, in fact, the most serious of the acute childhood diseases found in Britain, and can cause serious damage to the bronchi and lungs, or even death. It is particularly dangerous in premature babies.

One attack of the disease usually confers immunity to it for life, though there have been a few exceptions to this.

Incidence

Whooping cough mainly affects babies and infants, with around half of all cases occurring before the age of two. Adults can also be affected, though this rarely happens.

The introduction of routine vaccination against whooping cough in 1957 led to a dramatic drop in the number of cases in England and Wales, which fell from around 100,000 a year to a low of only 2,000 in 1972. The vaccine is not 100 per cent effective, however, and not all children are deemed to be suitable for vaccination.

In the early 1970s, there was considerable alarm concerning the safety of the whooping cough vaccine and a number of parents in Britain decided not have their children vaccinated. This meant that the proportion of children who were vaccinated fell to below 50 per cent around this time, and as a result the disease became much more common, with serious epidemics occurring every four years. Two particularly bad years, for example, were in 1978, when there were almost 70,000 recorded cases, and again in 1986, when there were 36,000 recorded cases.

Causes

Whooping cough is caused by a bacterium called *bordetella pertussis*, which infects the lungs, causing the airways to become clogged with a thick layer of mucus. It is transmitted by airborne droplets which are ejected into the air when the sufferer coughs, sneezes or speaks. There is an incubation period of between one and three weeks before the onset of symptoms.

Signs and Symptoms

The early symptoms of the illness are rather like those of a cold. It begins with a mild dry cough, a runny nose, sneezing, a slightly raised temperature and sore eyes which may be pink and watery. This is the most infectious period and the infected child should be kept away from other children. Unlike a cold, however, the symptoms do not improve after a few days but rather they get worse. The nasal discharge thickens and the cough will become aggravated, particularly at night, until it occurs more or less continuously in bouts lasting for up to a minute. Sudden attacks of coughing may follow one another in quick succession until the child expels a little sticky mucus and sinks back, exhausted by the effort. The child will probably also begin to 'whoop' at the end of each bout of coughing when gasping for breath. The noise is made by a sharp blast of air rushing through the half-open epiglottis, though this does not happen in all cases. A baby will whoop less loudly than an older child. The child will find it virtually impossible to breathe in during a bout of coughing, with the result that the face goes deep red and the tongue may protrude. During the paroxysmal stage of coughing, infectivity is slight. The cough may become so bad that it causes the child to vomit. In severe cases, the child may temporarily stop breathing after a coughing fit – this is known as apnoea.

The severe coughing phase of the disease can last from 2 to 10 weeks. It can be very distressing for the entire family, and very tiring for everyone especially if the coughing is particularly bad at night and parents and infant alike find it difficult to sleep. Gradually, the coughing will become milder and less frequent, though a weaker cough may last for several months.

Diagnosis

Whooping cough is generally diagnosed from observation of the symptoms. In case of doubt, however, the bacterium responsible can be grown from a pernasal swab, which is taken from the back of the nose, early on in the illness. This can confirm diagnosis.

Treatment

There is no effective treatment for whooping cough, especially once the coughing stage of the disease has started. A child who has whooping cough should stay in bed and be kept warm. Small, frequent meals should be given, preferably just after a coughing bout which will help reduce the chances of vomiting. Plenty of fluids should also be taken. Exposure to anything that may bring on fits of coughing, such as cigarette smoke or draughts, should be avoided.

During a coughing fit, a baby is more comfortable lying face down with the foot of the cot raised. Children often prefer to sit up and lean forwards. The doctor will probably visit regularly during the severe coughing stage of the illness. You should not give the child cough-suppressant medicines, as the cough, while distressing, serves the purpose of preventing mucus from clogging up the lungs.

If the illness is diagnosed early enough – that is before the coughing phase starts – a doctor may prescribe oral erythromycin, an antibiotic drug that will help reduce the child's infectivity to others. It may also reduce the duration of the illness.

If an infant becomes blue, this is known as cyanosis and indicates a serious lack of oxygen. If this happens at any time, or if your child is persistently vomiting after coughing fits, urgent admission to hospital is recommended, where the child will probably be given oxygen. This can be done either in a tent or by a face mask or a ventilator.

Complications

There are several complications that can arise from whooping cough. In general, the younger the child, the greater the risks, which can be fatal. Fatalities are very rare in children over the age of six months.

Severe coughing can cause nosebleeds, and bleeding from the blood vessels in the eyes. If the child vomits repeatedly, this can cause dehydration.

One of the most common complications affecting the chest may include acute bronchitis. Pneumonia is also common, when the lungs may be damaged permanently, and accounts for most of the deaths in infancy and old age. This affects about 1 child in 100 who has the disease. Other complications of the chest include a form of collapsed lung (known as pneumothorax) and permanent widening of the airways (a condition known as bronchiectasis). A radiograph should be carried out and appropriate physiotherapy taken if necessary.

Otitis media is another common infective complication. This is an inflammation of the middle ear and occurs as a result of infection extending up the Eustachian tube, which connects the back of the nose to the middle ear.

Yet another possible complication of whooping cough is the bursting of blood vessels in the brain, and encephalitis (swelling or inflammation of the brain cells). Encephalitis is heralded by drowsiness or sleepiness, when it is difficult to wake the child fully, accompanied by a headache, fear of bright lights, and sometimes unconsciousness. Encephalitis may cause seizures and coma, and can lead to mental impairment or death. This is a very serious condition and requires urgent medical attention.

Immunization

Most babies are vaccinated in the first year of life. It is usually given in a combined vaccine, with diphtheria and tetanus. In Britain, this is done at around three, five and nine months of age. The vaccine is not 100 per cent effective, though if the disease does occur in a child who has been immunized, that child is unlikely to be seriously ill with the disease. The vaccine should not be given to a baby who has a family or personal history of seizures, or who has a feverish illness or has suffered a reaction to a previous whooping cough vaccination. It used to be thought that children suffering from asthma or eczema should not be given the vaccine, because it was considered that the child could be at risk of having an allergic reaction to the constituents of the vaccine. The composition of modern vaccines has now been changed in order to remove this risk.

Side-effects of the vaccine may include redness and swelling at the site of the injection. There may also be a severe local swelling with marked tenderness, although this is rare, or a small, non-tender lump may persist for several weeks afterwards. The injection may cause an infant to become slightly feverish and out of sorts for a day or two. This is not considered to be a cause for concern, however. In very rare cases – around one in every 100,000 incidences – an infant may have a severe reaction, which may cause high-pitched, uncontrollable screaming or even seizures. A child aged between six months and five years may respond to a rapid rise of temperature by having a short fit, though this is very rare as a result of immunization. A child who is subject to epileptic fits may respond to the rise in temperature by having a fit, though this is also unusual.

In still rarer cases – about one in 300,000 – a baby may suffer permanent brain damage. This is the complication that has, not surprisingly, caused so much controversy in recent years. It is impossible to be precise about the incidence of brain damage resulting from immunization against whooping cough because it is impossible to say that the brain damage resulted from immunization as opposed to any other factors. However, one thing that it is possible to say, according to advocates of immunization, is that it is – from whatever cause – extremely rare.

Contraindications

The Department of Health in Britain advises against whooping cough immunization if a child has had fits in the past, or if there is a history of epilepsy or fits in the family, though this is not considered to be a contraindication in the USA or Scandinavia. The Department of Health also advises against immunization if the child suffered brain damage at birth.

One thing that all the experts agree on is that if a child has a fit shortly after immunization against whooping cough, a further injection should not be given.

Other contraindications include

- any acute infection
- any severe reaction to a previous whooping cough immunization, including a high fever, uncontrollable screaming for three hours or more, or a severe local reaction
- any degenerative disease of the nervous system

Risks Versus Benefits

The British Government continues to insist that whooping cough is a potentially dangerous disease and the risks of the illness are far higher than the dangers associated with the vaccine, which are minimal in comparison. In view of the seriousness of the disease, the Government maintains that it is important that as many babies who are suitable for vaccination be immunized. They estimate that the risk of encephalitis as a result of being immunized is three times less than that of encephalitis occurring as a complication of the disease itself. Advocates of immunization claim it is over 90 per cent effective and that the resulting immunity is thought to last for several years.

According to What Doctors Don't Tell You, scientists from the Institute of Medicine of the National Academy of

Science in America have recently admitted that the whooping cough part of DPT vaccine does damage some children. What Doctors Don't Tell You say that the risk could amount to as many as one in every 400 children. In testimony before the US Senate Committee in 1985, the then Secretary of Health, Edward Brandt Jr, estimated that each year some 35,000 children are brain damaged by this vaccine. The risks of the vaccine include encephalitis, meningitis, chronic neurological damage, Guillain-Barré syndrome, juvenile diabetes, learning disabilities, attention deficit disorder, and infantile spasms. Sudden Infant Death Syndrome (SIDS) has been shown in studies to affect children at eight times the normal rate within three days of being immunized.

In addition, a recent study at the University of California estimates that as many as one in every 13 babies responded to the DPT vaccine with persistent, high-pitched crying. It was thought that this may indicate minor neurological damage.

Dr Archie Kelokerinos, speaking at a Natural Health Convention in Stanwell Tops, New South Wales, in May 1987, had this to say about the whooping cough vaccine:

> The worst vaccine of all is the whooping cough vaccine ... It is responsible for a lot of deaths and for a lot of infants suffering irreversible brain damage. In susceptible infants, it knocks their immune systems about, leading to irreparable brain damage, or severe attacks or even deaths from diseases like pneumonia or gastro-enteritis and so on.

Justice for All Vaccine Damaged Children, an anti-vaccination pressure group, claims that the problem stems from the fact that the mass trials of whooping cough vaccine in Britain were designed to show its ability to prevent disease – not its safety. It states, quite unequivocally, 'there is no question that there is a risk' and urges parents to enquire about alternative means of protection.

According to What Doctors Don't Tell You, even the British government's resolve seems to be failing. According to *WDDTY* magazine in May 1995, government researchers are now admitting that the DPT vaccine can increase the risk of seizures five-fold.

Doubts have also been raised not only about the safety of the whooping cough vaccine but also about its efficacy. According to some health experts, the great decline in deaths from whooping cough occurred before the vaccine was introduced, and when there have been outbreaks of whooping cough, half or more of the sufferers had been fully vaccinated. According to Dr J. Anthony Morris, immunization expert formerly of the American Food and Drug Administration (FDA) and later of the Institute of Health and himself a believer in the whooping cough vaccine, it has only been between 63 and 93 per cent effective. That is a large variable and not a reassuring efficacy rate in relation to the risks involved.

Part Three:
Other Vaccinations

Foreign Travel

Immunization is often necessary before you travel abroad. It is, in any case, a requirement before entry into certain countries where particular diseases are prevalent. This is particularly true if you are going to the developing countries.

Anyone who is contemplating a journey should find out a few months before departure which immunizations are either necessary or recommended. You need to do this well in advance of your journey for several reasons. Firstly, some immunizations cannot be given at the same time. Secondly, some immunizations can take some time before they become effective. There may be a time lapse between immunization and protection, during which the body's immune system is stimulated into producing the necessary antibodies. One example of this is immunization against hepatitis B, which takes six months before it provides full protection.

If you need further information on immunization before you travel abroad, you can ask your doctor, your travel agent, or the Embassy or High Commission of the country concerned.

Major diseases

There are many serious diseases that are still prevalent in certain parts of the world and therefore present a risk to the traveller. Where it is possible, advocates of immunization will advise that you should always take what precautions you can against these diseases.

Malaria

Malaria is a major health problem throughout the tropics. It is a parasitic disease which is spread by the bites of infected mosquitoes. It causes fever and, in some cases, it can lead to certain complications which can affect the kidneys, liver, brain and blood. At its worst, it can be fatal.

People who are travelling to countries where malaria is endemic are recommended to ask their doctor about suitable anti-malaria medicines. Some areas are beset by malaria parasites that are resistant to anti-malaria medicines, so it is important to find out which medicine is the most suitable for you, depending on where you are going. The recommendation is to take the medicine after food for a week before travelling, throughout your stay, and for a month after your return.

What Doctors Don't Tell You warn against a number of toxic effects that anti-malaria tablets can have. These include 'nausea, vomiting, severe gastrointestinal disturbances and even psychotic reactions. Prolonged high doses of chloroquine can lead to damage to the cornea of the eyes or ringing of the ears.'

It is, of course, advisable to avoid being bitten by

mosquitoes by using insect repellent and a mosquito net at night.

What Doctors Don't Tell You recommend the use of a herb called Artemisia annua in China, or quinghao, or wormwood, in the West. According to What Doctors Don't Tell You, this herb has been recognized as an antimalarial drug in China since the early '70s. 'The Chinese have purified the herb, and in clinical trials of 2,000 patients, have demonstrated that this plant was more rapidly acting than any other animalarial agent, with no evident toxicity.

> So impressive is the action of this herb that it merited a laudatory editorial in *The Lancet* (14 March 1992) ... 'If you can get hold of an experienced Chinese herbalist, it might be prudent to take this herb, which has a better track record than most of the drugs now on the market.'

Rabies

This is an acute viral infection of the central nervous system and is transmitted via the bite of an infected animal. Symptoms include delirium and painful muscle spasms in the throat. If you are bitten by an animal, emergency medical treatment and the administration of a rabies vaccination should prevent the onset of symptoms. Once symptoms have developed, though, the disease is nearly always fatal.

Immunization against rabies is necessary only if you are likely to be exposed to an unusual risk of infection, or undertaking a long journey in a remote area where emergency medical treatment is unlikely to be available.

Immunization does not, however, prevent the need for urgent medical attention if you are bitten by an infected animal.

Bilharziasis

This is a parasitic disease, which is caused by a worm that is most commonly found in the waterways of Africa. If you are in a country where bilharziasis is prevalent, you should avoid wading or bathing in rivers, streams or lakes.

The worm penetrates the skin and can cause damage to the intestines, the liver and the urinary tract. The disease requires urgent medical attention. No vaccine is as yet available.

Cholera

This is an infection of the intestines. It is caught from contaminated food and water, and is a problem in countries with poor sanitation. It is common in South America, the Middle East, Africa and Asia. The disease can cause severe diarrhoea and may lead to dehydration and, in its extreme form, to death. It can be avoided by paying scrupulous attention to hygiene.

According to What Doctors Don't Tell You, it is now widely recognized that the cholera vaccine is of little value. This view was confirmed in the 5 July 1991 issue of *GP*, the newspaper sent to all general practitioners, when it said

Certain vaccines such as that given for cholera are known to be of no value, and the emphasis in general practice should really shift more towards proper advice, which can often be more time-consuming than injections.

This no doubt explains why the Department of Health booklet, *Health Advice for Travellers*, explains the situation in the following way:

A vaccine is available but it gives very little protection and is only recommended for travellers to cholera areas who may cross remote borders, especially overland, and may be asked for a certificate by checkpoint staff acting unofficially. No country now requires cholera immunization as an official condition of entry.

Dengue fever

Dengue fever is a virus transmitted by the female Aedes mosquito in parts of South America. It causes severe muscular pains, stomach inflammation, headache and haemorrhaging. It can be fatal. There is no treatment or vaccine available.

Diphtheria

This is a serious disease found in tropical countries, where there is poor hygiene, little sanitation and overcrowding. The disease has been virtually eradicated in developed countries but remains a problem in other parts of the world (*see also Part Two*).

Japanese encephalitis

This is a viral inflammation of the brain and can be life-threatening. It occurs throughout southeast Asia, particularly in rural areas and during the monsoon season. A vaccine is available and is recommended for travellers who are staying in high-risk areas for a month or longer. Immunization is not generally available under the National Health Service, and you will probably have to pay for it.

Meningococcal meningitis

This is a bacterial strain of meningitis, which is an inflammation of the membranes covering the brain and the spinal cord. It is prevalent in parts of Africa and Asia. A vaccine is available, but should not be confused with the vaccine that is available in Britain, which is against Haemophilus influenzae type b meningitis and is the form of bacterial meningitis that occurs most commonly in young children in Britain.

Polio

Polio is an infectious disease which can lead to paralysis. It is still prevalent in southern Europe, Africa and Asia, where the vaccine is not routinely available. This means that it is still a risk for people who have not been vaccinated and are travelling to those countries, in which case they should receive a full course of three doses of vaccine. People who were immunized over ten years ago are advised to take a booster injection.

What Doctors Don't Tell You accept that it may be prudent to consider polio immunization if you are travelling to high-risk areas at the height of summer, as most people under the age of 40 have not been exposed to the virus and will therefore not have built up a natural immunity to it. As for having a booster, though, What Doctors Don't Tell You say that 'you can ask to have a blood test to measure antibody response (serum titre) before you get a booster you don't need' (*see also Part Two.*)

Tetanus

This is a dangerous bacterial infection, which causes severe and painful muscle spasms and is transferred by the introduction of infected spores into the body through a wound. The spores are found mainly in soil and dirt. It is still a risk for people who have not been vaccinated and are travelling to remote countries, where medical treatment is not immediately available, in which case they are advised to receive a full course of three doses of vaccine. People who have been immunized over ten years ago are recommended to have a booster injection.

What Doctors Don't Tell You say that one of the problems with the tetanus immunization is that it has been purified to such an extent in order to prevent reactions to it that it is no longer as effective. In spite of this, What Doctors Don't Tell You claim that the tetanus vaccine can still cause high fever, pain, nerve damage to the inner ear, anaphylactic shock (which is a life-threatening allergic reaction), and degeneration of the nervous system. What Doctors Don't Tell You quote the *New England Journal of Medicine* as

Recommended vaccinations for foreign travel

Disease	Reason for Immunization	Effectiveness	Contraindications
Cholera	Sometimes compulsory for entry into certain countries in Asia and Africa. Also recommended for others.	Moderate protection for up to six months. Other precautions are also necessary in countries where there is cholera.	None
Diphtheria	Recommended for anyone who has not had childhood immunization.	Highly effective. A booster is needed every 10 years.	None
Hepatitis A	Recommended for anyone who is travelling to any country where standards of hygiene are low and sanitation is poor.	Moderate protection for up to three months. A booster is needed every five months during periods of prolonged travel or long-term residency.	None
Hepatitis B	Recommended for anyone who is at risk.	Highly effective.	None
Japanese encephalitis	Recommended for travellers to rural areas in southeast Asia.	Highly effective.	
Measles	Recommended for anyone who has not had childhood immunization or has not had measles.	Highly effective. Protection was thought to last a lifetime but recent outbreaks have led to new recommendations.	Fever, severe malnutrition, and active tuberculosis.

Disease	Recommendation	Effectiveness	Side-effects
Meningococcal meningitis	Recommended for anyone who is at risk, particularly travellers to some areas of Africa and Asia.	Highly effective.	None
Polio	Recommended for anyone who has not had childhood immunization.	Highly effective.	Severe diarrhoea and fever.
Rabies	Recommended for anyone who is at risk.	Highly effective.	None
Tetanus	Recommended for anyone who has not had childhood immunization, or who has not had a booster within the last 10 years.	Highly effective.	Acute febrile illness.
Tuberculosis	Recommended for anyone who has not had childhood immunization and is travelling to Asia, Africa, Central or South America, especially if you are going to be living closely with the indigenous population and are planning to stay for a month or longer.	Highly effective.	None
Typhoid fever	Recommended for ravel anywhere outside Europe, the USA, Canada, Australia and New Zealand.	Moderate protection for up to five years. A booster is then required. A booster is required every three years.	None
Yellow fever	Compulsory for entry into certain countries.	Highly effective for at least 10 years.	Vaccine should not be given to a child under one year old.

reporting, in 1981, that tetanus boosters can cause T-lymphocyte blood count ratios to plunge temporarily to below normal levels – similar to those found in sufferers from AIDS. 'Furthermore, according to the *Journal of American Medical Association* (14 November 1990), many patients react to thimerosol, the mercury-containing preservative used in the vaccine.' (*See also Part Two.*)

Tuberculosis

This is an infectious bacterial disease, which most commonly affects the lungs and can be fatal. If you have not been immunized against TB and are planning to stay for a month or longer in Asia, Africa, Central or South America, you are advised to be immunized, particularly if you are going to be living alongside the indigenous population rather than in an international hotel (*see also Part Two*).

Typhoid fever

Typhoid is an infectious bacterial disease contracted by eating contaminated food or drinking contaminated water. Immunization is generally recommended for anyone who is travelling outside northern Europe, North America, Australia and New Zealand. Immunization does not provide complete protection, so travellers are also recommended to drink water that has been boiled (and use this also to clean your teeth), or use bottled water, preferably sparkling water which is less likely to be tap water unofficially bottled. Take your own supply of chlorine- or iodine-based purification tablets which may be hard to buy on

your travels. Avoid eating ice-cream, shellfish, unpasteur-
ized dairy products, and fruit or salad unless it is peeled or
you have washed it yourself in boiled or bottled water.
Make sure all the food you eat is thoroughly cooked all the
way through, and try to avoid swallowing sea water.

Immunization against typhoid fever only provides
protection for up to three years. After that, travellers are
recommended to get a booster.

What Doctors Don't Tell You maintain that immunization against typhoid, as with cholera, is of limited value and
provides only minimal protection. They also say that the
side-effects, such as flu-type aches and muzziness, tend to
be worse in people over the age of 35, and that children
under one year old should not be given the vaccine.

Viral hepatitis

This is an infection of the liver which can cause jaundice.
There are two forms of the disease, hepatitis A and
hepatitis B.

Hepatitis A, which is also known as infectious hepatitis,
is usually caught by consuming contaminated food or
water. It occurs particularly in parts of Africa, Asia and the
Far East, including India. It can also be transmitted from
person to person as the virus is present in faeces, and poor
sanitation and hygiene encourage its spread. It is almost
always a mild disease in childhood but it is usually much
more severe in adults. The first symptoms are usually
those of a cold, including loss of appetite, an increase in
temperature, headache, nausea and sickness, followed by
the onset of jaundice. There is no treatment for infective

hepatitis, but an injection of Gamma globulin before travelling helps reduce the risk of infection.

Hepatitis B occurs all over the world and is spread in much the same way as HIV. In other words, it is spread through sexual contact, through sharing contaminated needles, and through transfusions of contaminated blood. A genetically engineered vaccine for hepatitis B is now available. It takes up to six months to become effective.

Yellow fever

This is caught from the bite of an infected mosquito and occurs in parts of Africa and South America. Some countries require a vaccination certificate before they will grant entry if you are travelling from an infected country.

What Doctors Don't Tell You accept that this is one immunization it may be impossible to avoid if you are going to places where you need a vaccination certificate. 'The vaccine,' they say 'which is given live, can cause encephalitis (inflammation of the brain), especially in children under nine months.'

Conclusion

Immunization has been practised for over a century, and for most of our children it is a routine practice which continues virtually unquestioned. Yet there is a small, but growing, minority of people who strenuously oppose the use of vaccines. Many of these people are parents who have refused to have their children vaccinated, and some are doctors who have refused to administer vaccines.

You will have seen, by now, what a very difficult subject this is. It is hard for the layman to understand the complex issues on both sides of the argument. The idea of setting out to control disease was obviously a good one. Whether it is still, in practice, a good one is another matter.

I hope that I have, at least, shed light on some of the issues involved in this difficult debate. There are no easy answers and the conclusions can only be drawn by you, after careful consideration and discussion with the health professionals in your life.

Bibliography

Curtis, Susan, *A Handbook of Homoeopathic Alternatives to Immunisation*, London, Winter Press, 1994

Gunn, Trevor, *Mass Immunization – A Point in Question*, Cumbria, Cutting Edge Publications

Illingworth, Ronald S., *The Normal Child – Some Problems of the Early Years and their Treatment*, Edinburgh, Churchill Livinstone, 1987)

Micklen, R.D., *The Disease, The Vaccine, The Homoeopathic Treatment*, Micklen, R.D., North View, Queensbury, Bradford. W. Yorks BD13 1LL, 01274 882847)

Miles, Martin, *Homoeopathy and Human Evolution*, London, Winter Press, 1992

Miller, Neil Z., *Vaccines – are they really safe and effective?*, National Vaccine Center, New Mexico, New Atlantean Press

Miller, Neil Z., *Immunization Theory vs. Reality*, New Mexico, New Atlantean Press

Sinclair, Ian, *Vaccination – The 'Hidden' Facts*, Sinclair, Ian, 5 Ivy Street, Ryde NSW 2112 Mobile 105 294 817, 1994)

Speight, Leslie J., *No.1 Concise Guide to Homoeopathy – Homoeopathy and Immunization*, Saffron Walden, Health Science Press

Useful Addresses

The Association of Parents of Vaccine Damaged Children
2 Church Street
Shipston-on-Stow
Warwickshire CV36 4AP
Tel: 01608 661595

British Airways travel clinics
Tel: 0171 831 5333 to find your nearest one

British Medical Association
BMA House
Tavistock Square
London WC1H 9JP
Tel: 0171 387 4499

The British Homoeopathic Association
27a Devonshire Street
London W1N 1RJ
Tel: 0171 935 2163

Dissatisfied Parents Together (DPT)
128 Branch Road
Vienna
VA22180
USA
Tel: 703–938–0342 or 703–938–3783

Health Education Authority
Hamilton House
Mabledon Place
London WC1H 9TX
Tel: 0171 383 3833

Hospital for Tropical Diseases
24-hour Travel Clinic Healthline
Tel: 0839 337733
(calls charged at 36p a minute cheap rate,
    48p a minute at all other times)

The Informed Parent
19 Woodlands Road
Harrow
Middlesex HA1 2RT
Tel: 0181 861 1022

The Institute for Complementary Medicine (ICM)
PO Box 194
London SE16 1QZ
Tel: 0171 237 5165

Justice Awareness and Basic Support (JABS)
1 Gawsworth Road
Golborne
Warrington WA3 3RF
Tel: 01942 713565

Justice for All Vaccine Damaged Children U.K.
Ivor & Enid Needs
Erins Cottage
Fussells Buildings
Whiteway Road
St. George
Bristol
BS5 7QY
Tel: 0117 955 7818

Medical Advisory Service for Travellers Abroad (MASTA)
24-hour Travellers' Health Line
Tel: 0891 224100
(calls charged at 36p a minute cheap rate,
    and 48p a minute at all other times)

The Trailfinders Clinic (London)
194 Kensington High Street
London W8 7RG
Tel: 0171 938 3999

The Trailfinders Clinic (Scotland)
254–284 Sauchiehall Street
Glasgow G2 3EH
Tel: 0141 353 0066

What Doctors Don't Tell You
4 Wallace Road
London NW1 2PG
Tel: 0171 354 4592

Index